ECUMENICAL STUDIES IN HISTORY
No. 11

REFORMATION VIEWS OF CHURCH HISTORY

by

GLANMOR WILLIAMS

JOHN KNOX PRESS
Richmond, Virginia

Published by Lutterworth Press, London, England, 1970
and John Knox Press, Richmond, Virginia, 1970

Standard Book Number: 8042-3835-9
Library of Congress Catalog Card Number: 70-107323

Printed in Great Britain

CONTENTS

	Page
PREFACE	5
I. THE CONTINENTAL BACKGROUND	7
II. THE ENGLISH PIONEER: WILLIAM TYNDALE	22
III. THE LINK: JOHN BALE	33
IV. THE CONSUMMATION: JOHN FOXE	46
V. AFTERMATH AND CONCLUSIONS	63
BIBLIOGRAPHY	75
NOTES	78
INDEX	82

3

ECUMENICAL STUDIES IN HISTORY

The purpose of this series is to examine afresh problems of Church History and to do this for the sake of Church Unity. The subjects are drawn from many periods, places and communions. Their unity lies not in a common outlook of the writers, nor in a common method of treatment. It lies solely in the aim of, in one way or another, directly or indirectly, furthering the unity of the Church. The contributors are no less diverse than the subjects, and represent many Churches, nations and races.

General Editors

THE REV. A. M. ALLCHIN, Pusey House, Oxford.

THE REV. MARTIN E. MARTY, PH.D., University of Chicago.

THE REV. T. H. L. PARKER, D.D., Oakington Vicarage, Cambridge.

Advisory Board

DR. G. V. BENNETT, New College, Oxford.

PROFESSOR OWEN CHADWICK, Selwyn College, Cambridge.

PRINCIPAL RUSSELL CHANDRAN, United Theological College, Bangalore, S. India.

PROFESSOR HORTON DAVIES, Princeton University, U.S.A.

FATHER B.-D. DUPUY, O.P., Catholic Theological Faculty, Le Saulchoir, Paris.

PROFESSOR CHARLES FORMAN, Yale Divinity School, U.S.A.

FATHER BERNARD LEEMING, S.J., Heythrop College, Chipping Norton, England.

PROFESSOR J. D. MCCAUGHEY, Ormond College, Melbourne, Australia.

PROFESSOR JAMES MACEWEN, University of Aberdeen, Scotland.

PROFESSOR HARRY SAWYERR, University College, Sierra Leone.

PROFESSOR JAMES SMYLIE, Union Theological Seminary, Richmond, Virginia, U.S.A.

PROFESSOR RICHARD STAUFFER, Protestant Theological Faculty, Paris.

PROFESSOR BENGT SUNDKLER, Uppsala University, Sweden.

PREFACE

THE SUBSTANCE of this volume was originally delivered as the Whitley Trust Lectures for 1965. I should like to record my gratitude to the Trustees for the honour they did me in inviting me to be the Whitley Trust Lecturer in that year. I should also like to thank the Reverend Principals Dykes and Russell of the Northern Baptist College and the Reverend Dr. E. A. Payne and Dr. Roger Thomas for the kind arrangements they made for me when the lectures were delivered in Manchester and London respectively. I am also grateful to Dr. L. G. Champion, Secretary to the Trust, and his successor, Dr. B. R. White, for much kindness and consideration.

In preparing this volume I have modernized the spelling and punctuation of the titles of sixteenth-century books and of the quotations taken from them. The bibliography gives details of the original titles and dates of publication.

I am particularly indebted to the Reverend Dr. T. H. L. Parker of Cambridge, one of the editors of this series. He read my typescript with great care and thoroughness. His learning and perspicacity saved me from errors and revealed to me obscurities and fallacies in my argument. I have benefited much from his friendly advice and criticism.

Two friends have greatly contributed to clarifying and enriching my understanding of the sixteenth-century reformers and their view of history. Frank Smith Fussner, of Reed College, Portland, Oregon, sharply stimulated my thinking when he published his fine book, *The Historical Revolution*. His conversation did even more for me when he spent the academic session of 1964–65 at the University College of Swansea as visiting Fulbright Professor. My colleague, Ieuan Gwynedd Jones, Professor of Welsh History at Aberystwyth, and I have for many years had a common interest in the Reformation and its historiography. I hope it has been a two-way exchange between us, but on my side I am conscious of incurring a serious deficit in the "balance of payments".

Finally I have, as always, to record my deepest gratitude to my wife for her unfailing help, patience and encouragement.

Glanmor Williams

Swansea,
September 1967

5

I

THE CONTINENTAL BACKGROUND

LOOKING BACK over a century of upheaval and revolution in theology and scholarship, the English philosopher-statesman, Francis Bacon, with his accustomed percipience, rightly pointed to the effect which Martin Luther had had upon the study of the past. He had been obliged, Bacon argued, "to awake all antiquity and to call former times to his succours . . . so that the ancient authors both in divinity and humanity, which had a long time slept in libraries, began generally to be read and resolved".[1]

This was not because Luther would have regarded himself as a historian. Certainly it was not because he based his doctrine primarily on a study of the past. On the contrary, his convictions sprang from an agonizing personal experience in the present and an intense and searching meditation on the Scriptures. It was they, not any awareness of history, which gave birth to his passionate sensitivity to an individual relationship between God and man; to the sinner's desperate need for grace, to his redemption not by any external act or works prescribed by the Church or devised by the imagination of man but by an inward act of faith responding to the inscrutable mystery of divine grace. He found all this in himself and in the Word, and not in any historical works or chronicles. And he was convinced, with the single-minded faith of a man who believed himself transported from the unimaginable despair and isolation of the God-deserted to the ecstatic liberty of the God-redeemed, that did he but convey to others his experience they must inevitably share a heavenly rapture which was so real to him.

But—and this is the point where we at once begin to see the force of Francis Bacon's comment—almost as soon as Luther came to communicate his sensibilities to others he began to realize that defenders of orthodoxy would denounce them as an intolerably presumptuous threat on the part of a single misguided monk to fifteen hundred years of established authority in the Church. In the famous Leipzig debates of 1519 Luther's opponent, John Eck, quickly sensed—more swiftly and clearly than Luther himself at first—what the implications of the

7

reformer's views on papal supremacy were. Eck asserted that the pope's position of primacy was of divine origin: "The Holy Roman and Apostolic Church obtained the primacy not from the Apostles but from our Lord and Saviour himself, and it enjoys pre-eminence of power above all of the churches and the whole flock of Christian people."[2] In reply to this and similar arguments Luther was forced to deny the historical origin and continuity of power which Eck claimed for the papacy. Luther's fundamental counter-argument was his scriptural exegesis, but he was not content to rely solely on this. Even now he advanced an historical argument, based on the Early Fathers, the great church councils, and such historical authors as Platina who had written a well-known *Lives of the Popes*, published in 1479, in order to prove his own contention that the papal primacy was a phenomenon of human, not to say diabolical, inspiration and one of comparatively recent development in many respects. In the course of the next twenty or thirty years, Luther's conviction of the value of the historical arguments was greatly strengthened. Thus in 1535, in a preface to the *Vitae Pontificum* published in Wittenberg by the Englishman, Robert Barnes, he could write:

> I for my part, unversed and ill-informed as I was at first with regard to history, attacked the papacy, *a priori*, as they say, that is out of the Holy Scriptures. And now it is a wonderful delight to me to find that others are doing the same thing *a posteriori*, that is from history—and it gives me the greatest joy and satisfaction to see, as I do most clearly, that history and Scripture entirely coincide in this respect.

"That history and Scripture entirely coincide in this respect!"—we could easily take this to be the essential keynote of all those views of history that are subsequently to be discussed in this volume.

But the implications of Luther's appeal to history could look very different to other eyes. Quite apart from the counter-arguments raised by a clerical controversialist like Eck, there was the obvious and very serious objection voiced by an intelligent layman like the Emperor Charles V: "For it is certain", he protested, "that a single monk must err if he stands against the opinion of all Christendom. Otherwise Christendom itself would have erred for more than a thousand years."[3] Charles summed up the reactions of a great many of his contemporaries. His were reservations which might give pause even to a man of temperament as leonine and beliefs as white-hot as Luther's. And Luther himself had doubts from time to time on this score—he would

8

have been less than human if he had not! While he was in the Wartburg Castle, his "Isle of Patmos" as he termed it, in hiding after the Diet of Worms, destructive doubts assailed him. "Are you alone wise?" he nagged himself. "Have so many centuries gone wrong? What if you are in error and are taking so many others with you to damnation?"[4] He overcame these perplexities, but they were to return many times before the end of his life. Nor need we wonder at such misgivings that all the history of Christendom might be testifying against him. The boldest minds in the sixteenth century shuddered at the prospect of breaking with established authority. None cared to pose as a revolutionary; every innovator, however radical, disguised the fact from himself and his contemporaries by seeking to present his ideas as a return to the truth: Utopia must be found in Eden.

That Luther should suffer a crisis of confidence from time to time at the thought of rejecting the all-pervasive influence and jurisdiction of the Church should not surprise us. He was emboldened to make the break, however, because he believed he was appealing to a still higher fount of authority—the Word of God. In the first and last resort, he and every other Protestant reformer believed that a challenge as daring and disruptive as they were offering was justified by an overriding need to bring about a reversal of priorities in contemporary religion: to give it a God-inspired authority in place of a man-centred one.

The appeal, then, was primarily to the nature of the relationship between God and man as revealed in the Scriptures. There, too, would be found the authentic pattern established by the divine founder of Christianity for continuing his purpose of revealing God's intentions for men among succeeding generations. But what if, as Luther claimed, the faith had become by his time obscured and distorted by the inventions of men? What if the Church, as it existed in the sixteenth century, was a hindrance, indeed an enemy, to truth? Then it followed it must be of crucial interest and value to sincere Christians to learn when, where and why the Church had come to depart from the pattern laid down by its founder. The stark and startling contrast, as it seemed to the reformers, between the Church of the Apostles and that ruled over by the contemporary popes would be *justified* by the appeal to the Scriptures. It would be *explained* by the appeal to history.

It was this which accounted for Luther's growing regard for the testimony of history. He was not a historian, nor a humanist, still less an intellectual system-builder. But he was capable of some remarkable historical insights; and he had an implicit view of history more significant and compelling than has often been supposed. It has recently been the subject of careful analysis. These studies may, in the nature of the case, have given Luther's view of history more shape and coherence than ever they assumed in the tempestuous and often inchoate writings of the reformer himself. But they do establish conclusively the value and importance of Luther's intuitive recognition of the importance of the historical process as interpreted by the Christian, both for his own and subsequent generations of reformers.

However, there were other major Continental reformers who were in many respects even more concerned with the historical implications of their doctrine than Luther. Some of them had a better equipment in humanist training than he. As such, they were more drawn to the study of early texts, particularly to the writings of the great Latin and Greek Fathers. In Luther's own church his colleague, Melanchthon, particularly appreciated the value of the doctrine of the early Church, which he was very fond of regarding as *ecclesia doctrix*, the teaching church. Some of the great Swiss reformers were also steeped in the learning and methods of the humanists. One may be specially picked out; not because he was by any means the greatest among them but because of the particular influence he wielded among reformers in England. This was Heinrich Bullinger, Zwingli's successor at Zurich and author of a very voluminous correspondence with a large number of English reformers who looked, and not in vain, to this wise and moderate Swiss leader for guidance and counsel in all matters spiritual. Bullinger also published a series of fifty sermons in five parts of ten each in a book called *The Decades* which was greatly admired and widely read in England. In his fifth and last decade, where he treats of the nature of the Church, Bullinger brings out most sharply the contrast, as he saw it, at all points between the true Church founded on the warrant of scriptural truth and that of the papists, dependent in so many vital points on human tradition. Of their attitude in this context Bullinger wrote:

> But they do know well enough that the chief points of popery can be proved with no expressed scripture, or with reasons deducted out of the Scripture; therefore they feign unwritten matters, or traditions that were never written, whereby they may clout up and supply fitly that which they see want in the Scripture, and cannot be proved thereby. . . . To be short, whatsoever the whole Church of Rome hath hitherto kept shall be a tradition, although it be neither found, nor painted, nor written anywhere in any book canonical, yea although it be quite contrary to the Scripture. And so that shall be a tradition what they list.[5]

Hence the urgency, in Bullinger's eyes, of bringing to light how these "traditions" had been successively devised and introduced.

Bullinger's *Decades* was very similar in the general treatment of its argument to an infinitely greater and more influential book, Calvin's *Institutes of the Christian Religion*. Calvin, like Bullinger, treats of the nature of the Church in the last section of his book, but argues his case with much greater concentration and intellectual power. It was typical of Calvin that his conversion to the reformers' view of the Church should have been a slow and deliberate process. Admittedly he says in his preface to his Commentary on the Psalms that his final decision to leave the church of his upbringing was sudden. That may have been so; but it was only the last step in a long and gradual realization that the reformers' doctrines which had at first so shocked him by their apparent novelty and heresy were in reality those of the pristine Church of the New Testament from which the Church of Rome had turned away. The nature of Calvin's conversion explains much about his subsequent teaching. He grasped more readily than any of the other reformers the importance of the visible Church. His was a generation when, in Germany and Switzerland, much of the impulse of the reformed churches was being enervated and dissipated, when the Roman Church was re-forming its ranks and burnishing its weapons. To counter this, Calvin emphasized that if the Reformed Church was ever to replace Rome, or even successfully to defend itself against counter-attack, it must seek to create within itself the three sources of strength possessed by its great enemy: unity, authority and universality. But it meant also that the line between the true Church and the false Church must be drawn in the sharpest and clearest way. That was why, in the fourth and last book of the *Institutes*, the gulf which Calvin saw between the true Church founded on scriptural authority and the false Church based on the authority of Rome was so brilliantly demonstrated.

Stage by stage, with remorseless logic, Calvin defined the Church as its founder conceived it, and contrasted this with the distortions and perversions introduced and authorized by the papacy. He began by considering the rule or government of the Church. In chapter IV he outlined the state of the Church, "as this will give us a kind of visible representation of the divine institution". Then in chapter V this was followed by an account of how "the ancient form of government was utterly corrupted by the tyranny of the papacy". Chapters VI and VII developed historically the theme of the rise of the papacy "till it attained a height by which the liberty of the Church was destroyed and

11

all true rule overthrown". He proceeded similarly to show how the "unbridled licence" of the papal Church had corrupted doctrine, legislation and jurisdiction. Calvin had a remarkable knowledge of the Early Fathers' works and other early records of the Church, and he brought to the interpretation of them the skill, in the highest degree, of an expert jurist and erudite humanist. He was endowed, in addition, with a keen sense of history:

> If there were no records, men of sense would judge from the nature of the case that . . . a mass of rites and observances did not rush into the Church all at once, but crept in gradually. For though the venerable bishops who were nearest in time to the Apostles introduced some things pertaining to order and discipline, those who came after them, and those after them again, had not enough of consideration, while they had too much curiosity and cupidity, he who came last always vying in emulation with his predecessors, so as not to be surpassed in the invention of novelties.[6]

At all points, Calvin held his own clear and coherent view of the true Church over and against the Roman Church which had superseded it. He defined the contrast in sharp clear-cut lines with no loose edges. And he coupled with it a categorical imperative that all the accumulated dross of the dark ages of papal usurpation be removed and the true Church restored in all its original purity. Calvin, like many another creative Christian thinker, derived much of his force from his unfaltering certainty that the consummation of human destiny lay *beyond* history; but he also cherished a superb confidence that it was both possible and necessary to realize God's will *within* history.

Naturally, in the heat of the bitter religious controversies which took place between 1517 and 1560, many of the arguments and much of the evidence used by Protestants to substantiate their view of church history were scattered widely and haphazardly in a variety of books and pamphlets. In the 1550s an attempt was made to bring this material together into a synthesis. The result was the famous work of Protestant historiography known as the *Centuries of Magdeburg*. Published in thirteen volumes between 1559 and 1574, it was the work primarily of the Lutheran, Matthias Flacius Illyricus. Each volume covered a century of history, and the controlling theme of the work was that secular history is the scene of an unending conflict between God and the Devil, between Christ and Anti-Christ, represented here as the papacy. The publication of the work was preceded by an intensive search for materials which produced a veritable arsenal of arguments on which

Protestants could draw in their attacks on Catholic opponents. Throughout there was a heavy Protestant bias, frequently uncritical in its approach to sources. But for all its limitations—in some respects because of them—the book became tremendously influential. It gave a new impetus to church history, not merely among reformers but in the Roman Church also. "The very method of the attack—the use of history to destroy the basis of justification for an ancient institution—was a stimulus to the study and development of historical research. The Catholics could not permit the attack to go unchallenged and were compelled to turn to history to find ammunition for a counter-offensive."[7] The upshot was the equally famous and influential Catholic book, Cardinal Baronius's *Annales Ecclesiastici* (1588–1607).

So far, the attempt has been made to indicate various ways in which some of the Protestant leaders were driven to formulate their own appeal to history. It would not be possible, even if it were desirable, to subject the views of all the major reformers to detailed individual analysis. A more profitable approach may be to try to present first of all some of their general assumptions about the nature of history and then to examine how they proceeded to apply them to gain an understanding of the history of the Christian Church in Europe.

First, these reformers shared with many other Christians before their time and since an unshakeable conviction of the Christian meaning of history. Of all the great religions of mankind none has so central or so pervasive a sense of history as Christianity. It claims to link the events of terrestrial history to the immutable eternal scheme of things. It professes to unfold the whole of the mighty cosmic sequence enacted beyond and within history. It is grounded in the unique historical circumstances of the life of Christ. This is the pivot on which turns everything that happened before and everything which is to befall after.

Again, the reformers laid particular emphasis on the unique authority of the Scriptures as the source of revelation of this historical *schema*. The Bible was in many senses a history, but a history of a very remarkable kind. It was a history in which the intervention of God was seen on virtually every page. He was no remote and impersonal first cause; no detached, capricious or cynical Olympian observer. He was a direct participant unmistakably revealing his will and his reactions in a highly personal—it might almost be said, human—way. Scriptural example was reinforced by the attitudes of the two most influential authors of Christian history, Eusebius and Augustine. Both taught the same moral:

that God intervened regularly in human affairs and, more important still, that his interventions followed an unmistakable and traceable pattern.

That brings us next to consider how that pattern appeared to the eyes of the reformers. They shared fully the biblical awareness of a covenant between God and his people. If it is permissible to put it in such terms, God went in very much for "stick and carrot" diplomacy in his relations with men. When the people were faithful to him and obeyed his injunctions they were blessed and rewarded. Conversely, when they went whoring after false gods they brought down condign punishment on their heads. To take but one example from the writings of the Welsh Puritan martyr, John Penry. He firmly believed that if the Elizabethan Church did not mend its ways after a Puritan fashion, God might use the military might of Spain as an instrument of his wrath to punish the English nation for its tardiness in reforming religion. Punishment might, then, take a material or physical form. But infinitely worse retribution in the view of the reformers was that of a spiritual kind: that God allowed the light of his gospel to become obscured so that men were in danger of everlasting darkness. The Church itself, the very instrument devised by God for ensuring that his truth should continue to be preached to mankind, could, as a punishment for men's wickedness, be subverted by their adversary, the Devil, and become the tool of Anti-Christ. Such a view of history necessarily heightened the tension of the moral drama of the struggle being waged between cosmic powers in an earthly arena and lent it a significance far beyond that of any contest on the purely terrestrial or secular plane.

Given the reformers' view of the incorrigibly sinful nature of unregenerate man they might have been led to near-despair. They were saved from this by their still greater emphasis on the infinite mercy of divine grace and the ultimately irresistible power of the divine will. However much the powers of evil might appear to triumph, however completely Anti-Christ might seem to have the whole Church within his grasp, divine providence ensured that Satan would never become entire master. The light of truth was never entirely extinguished; the faithful were never wholly destroyed. Always in every age, no matter how dark, there was a saving remnant. There was always a hope of restoration. It was characteristic that Luther should entitle one of his earliest and most famous tracts, *On the Babylonish Captivity of the Church*. Implicit in it was the idea not only that the Church had for long been in captivity to the enemies of God but also that he would no less surely free it in the fullness of time. He would allow the reformers, like Nehemiah, to rebuild the walls of Jerusalem.

All this was, inescapably, not a philosophy of history but a theology of history. It was a manifesto of God's ways with men down the ages; the working out of human affairs in conformity with the divine will and purpose. It was not only a theology of history but hardly less a history of theology; an account of how men had forwarded or thwarted a revelation of the true knowledge of God. It was, therefore, sacred or ecclesiastical history; an examination of decisive phases in the history of the Church conceived of as a series of fateful choices. The age-old notion of cataclysmic events leading to strongly defined phases of history was still very much present. Equally vivid was the consciousness of an historic choice awaiting contemporaries. The reformers had no doubt that a long dark phase in the history of the Church was over and that restoration of the true Church was possible. Such a cataclysmic view of the past, however unhistorical it may now appear, could be wonderfully potent in releasing energy and confidence in the present.

Given this much simplified but not, it is hoped, distorted conceptual framework of history within which the reformers worked, it may now be worth trying to see how they applied it to the church history in which they were interested. Before proceeding to try to answer that question, however, it is important to recognize, as many historians have recently come to do, that there is a valid and necessary distinction to be drawn between two major groups of reformers. These groups have been conveniently categorized by American historians as Magisterial Reformers and Radical Reformers. By the Magisterial Reformers is generally meant all those who believed that a state Church or an established Church could be justified. This would include Lutherans, Calvinists and Anglicans. The term Radical Reformers refers to those who, whatever other differences existed between them, rejected a state Church and held only to gathered congregations of believers, e.g. Anabaptists, Spiritualists and Evangelical Rationalists. It would be out of place here to embark upon an extended examination of the latter. But it is not unfair to comment that the value of their contribution to the Reformation has been increasingly recognized in recent years. It need hardly be added that their viewpoint, often misunderstood and even travestied in the past, has a particular interest for those who belong to the Nonconformist tradition.

Taking the Magisterial Reformers first, we find among them many differences of detail and emphasis. But for our present purpose these can be ignored in concentrating upon those key ideas common to them all. First of all, they believed firmly that the touchstone by which the purpose and nature of the Church must be judged was scriptural authority. In the Bible was to be found the authentic revelation of what God himself had intended his Church to be, committed to writing by the only "sure and warranted ammanuenses of the Holy Spirit", as Calvin called the writers of the Bible. In this context we may recall Luther's insistence upon Scripture as the Word of God in contra-distinction to the words of men. Most other reformers followed him in this. God had spoken and made plain his intentions. If anything had gone amiss with the Church it was obviously because the Word had become obscured and misinterpreted by the agency of man. Hence the indispensable need to strip away all such dross in order to recover the pure gold of God's truth. Men must rediscover what Christ had laid down for his followers. How had those followers believed and wor-shipped? What was the Church like in the time of the Apostles and how could it be restored in the sixteenth century? But rediscovery and restoration were nothing like as easy in practice as they at first appeared. What the New Testament had to say was limited and fragmentary. Reformers might insist in theory that it was open only to one inter-pretation, yet in practice they often found themselves sharply divided in their understanding of it. Two key questions which immediately arose were, first, was the character of the Church of the Apostles as a small minority of persecuted missionary enthusiasts entirely adaptable to the very changed conditions of sixteenth-century Christendom? Secondly, was the authority of the Bible to be applied in such a way as to exclude everything from the Church which was not specifically warranted by scriptural authority or in such a way as to include many things which were not specifically forbidden by scriptural texts?

Reformers were therefore obliged from the outset to supplement their study of the New Testament by a close historical survey of the Church of the post-apostolic age, the Church of the Early Fathers. The attitude of the reformers towards the Fathers was revealing. In general, of course, they were profoundly respectful and approbatory. There were some of the Fathers, notably Augustine, who were particularly dear to them. But even the Fathers were not wholly blameless, the reformers thought. The weakness they saw was that even at this early stage human inventions and glosses could creep in and endanger the authority of the Scriptures. Some of the weeds that had so freely flourished later in the medieval Church had first germinated in the early period. Yet, by and large, the Reformers were agreed that for the first five hundred years of its history the Church, though not entirely unblemished, had succeeded in maintaining intact the essentials of apostolic purity of doctrine, worship and organization.

What, then, had gone wrong and who had been responsible for it? Briefly, the authority of the Scriptures had been displaced; and the instrument of wickedness had been the papacy. Not that the papacy had been always and wholly corrupt. Even Gregory the Great, often regarded by modern historians as the father of the medieval papacy, found some favour in the eyes of the reformers. Bullinger, for instance, referred with warm approval to Gregory's comment: "I affirm boldly that whosoever he be that calleth himself the universal priest is a forerunner of Anti-Christ."[8] The real turning-point had come with the relations between the Emperor Phocas and Pope Boniface III. Phocas was the worthless adventurer who successfully led a rebellion against the Eastern Emperor Maurice and deposed him, becoming in the process the first usurper to occupy the imperial throne at Constantinople. It was Phocas, said Calvin, "who conceded to Boniface III what Gregory by no means demanded—that Rome should be head of all churches".[9] This opened a phase of five hundred years in which "the tyranny of the Roman bishop was established, and ever and anon increased". With the ascendancy of Hildebrande in the eleventh century a still more disastrous phase of five hundred years opened, culminating in all the abuses of the sixteenth century which the reformers so fiercely excoriated.

But still they maintained that the darkness of these centuries, though gross, had not been total. Beneath the bushel with which the truth was covered there burned the tiny lamp of the invisible Church of true believers. The major reformers always insisted that it was impossible for men to separate the invisible Church from the visible one. Whatever the corruptions of the visible Church, the invisible was always included within it. "The Church continued as it always had in the main stream of the divine operation—the Church must always exist under, amidst, and even in the possession of its adversaries."[10] The Magisterial Reformers were at all times anxious to dissociate themselves from any suggestion that their invisible Church was to be identified with heresy. This was a charge to which they were always peculiarly sensitive and always wanted to rebut. On the other hand, of course, when it came to comparatively recent heretics like Wycliffe or Huss they were not unwilling to recognize that these men had stood up valiantly for truth and had, in some important respects, anticipated their own teaching.

Finally, these reformers were deeply convinced that the overpowering force of God-in-history had not ceased to work in their own time. Indeed, their own generation had been given the most striking manifestation of divine intervention; an intervention designed to reverse the downward plunge which the Church had taken for a thousand years, to punish Anti-Christ, and to restore the Church to its true apostolic lineaments. With their acute sense of successive "ages" of history, the reformers were convinced that the Reformation had opened a new phase in the history of the Church in which the hand of God could work inexorably for good. But it laid upon them an awe-inspiring obligation to ensure that they lent themselves to what they conceived to be his will.

Turning from the Magisterial Reformers to the Radical Reformers, we find that they shared most of the views that we have already attributed to the former, but they held them with a greater degree of intensity. In each instance the Radicals would have held that the Magisterial Reformers would not face up to the full implications of their own doctrines, that they were "half-way men" who stopped far short of the whole truth. So, to take first of all their attitude towards the nature of the Church as revealed in the Scriptures. The Radicals were inclined to a more fully literal interpretation of the New Testament. They wanted the Church of the sixteenth century to resemble in all respects that of the Apostles, i.e. a gathered and disciplined congregation of voluntary believers; an ardent missionary minority propagating its beliefs without support from or connexion with the State—most likely, indeed, in the teeth of opposition to it.

Hence their emphasis on adult baptism, not so much for its own sake but as a symbol of conscious, voluntary adult acceptance of the teaching, obligations and discipline of a gathered congregation of Christian believers. It was on this question of adult baptism that Magisterial Reformers found themselves in greatest embarrassment when in controversy with Radicals. For it was not easy to counter the argument that, judged by scriptural text, precedent and ethos alone, the Radicals appeared to be closer than the Magisterials to the Apostles' view of the Church.

Similarly, the two groups differed widely over the application to

18

their own time of apostolic teaching and practice in relation to the "great commission", i.e. St. Matthew 28: 19–20: "Go ye therefore and teach all nations, baptizing them in the name of the Father and of the Son and of the Holy Ghost.", or St. Mark 16: 15–16: "Go ye into all the world and preach the Gospel to every creature. He that believeth and is baptized shall be saved." The Radicals believed that such an injunction was as valid and as necessary for the Church in their own day as it had been for the Apostles.

Other issues on which they were inclined to take a similarly literalist view were the communism of goods, the swearing of oaths, and non-resistance to evil.

Having on these counts a view of the New Testament Church far more drastically antithetical to the medieval Church than had the Magisterial Reformers, the Radical Reformers had necessarily arrived at a correspondingly more pessimistic assessment of the "fall of the Church" from the pristine apostolic standards. They also offered a rival explanation and chronology of it. Whereas the Magisterial Reformers saw the emergence of the papacy as the *fons et origo* of all evils, most of the Radicals fathered the responsibility on the Emperor Constantine, who first brought about that unholy alliance of State and Church which had been the real source of contamination. "The Christian emperor seemed to them the very culmination of worldliness and power consciousness. Among the Anabaptists the special mark of the fall was the union of Church and State and the use of the civil arm in matters of faith."[11]

Most of the Radicals were captivated by Eusebius's record of the history of the Christian Church before Constantine: the persecuted minority suffering at the hands of a hostile and worldly State—so similar to their own condition; and yet exhibiting an unforgettable instance of power in weakness—so evocative of hope for them! But there were still more drastic views of the fall than this among a minority of Anabaptists, some of whom believed it had taken place in the immediate post-apostolic age.

Though the Radicals did not regard the rise of the papacy as being as decisive a downward turn in the history of the Church as did the Magisterials, in some ways they held it in even greater detestation, because they saw in the rise of Rome the worst possible combination of Church and State, in which the Church, not content with allying itself to the power of the State, went still further and arrogated temporal jurisdiction to itself. The result, in Radical eyes, in terms of corruption by wealth and worldly power and the pursuit of ends utterly opposed to those of the true Church, could not fail to be calamitous. That the papacy was Anti-Christ they had no doubt, any more than did most of the Magisterial Reformers. But some among the Radicals were much more widely embracing in their view of Anti-Christ. Most notable was Sebastian Franck who, in his *Chronica*, included not only the papacy and the infidel but even reformers, including Luther, who did not share his views.

When it came to tracing the history of the invisible Church of true believers during the long centuries of evil domination and darkness the Radicals found themselves in sharp disagreement with the Magisterial Reformers. Because the unholy alliance of Church and State from the Age of Constantine onwards had made for the negation of all that they understood by the Christian Church, the Radicals held it to be utterly unthinkable that true believers could have been comprehended within the utterly corrupt state Church. During the thousand years and more of darkness, the true Church was in dispersion among those called heretics. The succession of the saving remnant was to be traced back from Huss, Wycliffe, to the Fraticelli, the Waldensians and other much more obscure believers persecuted and dubbed heretics by the papal Church. There were even those among them who went so far as to argue that the succession of true belief had been broken off almost immediately after the age of the Church of the Apostles itself.

Finally, parallel with the variance concerning the past went an equally sharp divergence on the nature of the restitution of the scriptural Church in the present. The more adamant Radical insistence became upon the distinctive characteristics of the New Testament Church, the wider became the chasm seen to separate it from the papal Church and the more imperative the call for its complete restitution. The more emphatic their assertion that past and present experience showed that it was the link between Church and State which was the cause of all perversion, the more indispensable it became to free the Church completely from any association with the lay power. The Radicals constantly chided other reformers with shrinking from the full consequences of their own doctrine and with resting content with half-hearted restoration of the Church. The Radicals claimed that for their part they wanted complete restitution whereas other reformers would go no further than reformation.

Despite the many contradictions and differences of emphasis among the various kinds of reformers, there is no doubt that their general view of history had an immense potential appeal. Particularly was this true of the Calvinist view of history which became the most widely accepted in northern Europe and in north America. It was one which was to be unusually persuasive among English-speaking reformers with whom we shall be especially concerned. It reinforced in the most coherent, persuasive and militant fashion the theology of the Protestant Reformation. It made still more articulate the longings and aspirations of many who had been gradually learning to form and voice opinions for themselves. It provided a world-view of historical destiny and church history peculiarly sympathetic to many of them. It supplied a rationale for the disgust and revulsion many of them had come to feel for the widely admitted excesses of the late medieval Church. The authority which upheld such abuses was itself believed to be, historically, a usurpation anyway. Moreover, it offered a reasoned rejection of the whole sacerdotal basis which had developed in the medieval Church.

The clerical pretensions of the Middle Ages had been such as almost to restrict the usage of the term "Church" to cover the ecclesiastical hierarchy only. Certainly they had created a situation in which the clergy appeared to be the only "first-class citizens" of the City of God, with the laity very much "second-class citizens". This state of affairs could now be depicted as having come about contrary to the divine intention; an incubus foisted on the Church by human greed for wealth and power. Furthermore, Calvinist historiography elevated the lay vocation. It made a reality within the visible Church of the priesthood of true believers and the spiritual liberty of the Christian man.

And finally, it inculcated the notion of the elect; a notion wonderfully reassuring in its psychological consolation and amazingly productive of spiritual energy. Added to which this was a notion suffused by Old Testament conditioning which could be applied almost as easily to a nation as to an individual.

II

THE ENGLISH PIONEER: WILLIAM TYNDALE

ON OCTOBER 31, 1517, the then obscure friar-professor, Martin Luther, had pinned up his ninety-five arguments on the church door at Wittenberg. He was, unbeknown to himself, proclaiming doctrines which were to find an echo in all corners of Europe in a remarkably short space of time. Among those who were most gladly to receive and propagate the Lutheran message was a young Englishman, William Tyndale, the outstanding English reformer of the first generation and a major figure among English reformers of any generation.

Tyndale was born probably about 1491 or 1492 somewhere in or near the Marches of Wales, possibly indeed on the western bank of the River Severn and not, as used to be thought, on its eastern bank. He went up to the university of Oxford in 1506 and remained there until 1519 when he migrated to Cambridge. There he stayed until 1521. In that year Luther's books were publicly burned at the university and young Tyndale may have decided that the atmosphere there had become too uncongenial, if not indeed positively dangerous, for him. It is not certainly known when, where or from whom he received the new reforming doctrines. But it seems reasonable to assume that he had done so at the university. What is more important is that, having encountered them, he should so readily and wholeheartedly have embraced them. In the words of one of his biographers, Demaus:

> One thing is certain, the seed of Protestantism however or whenever sown, took deep root in his mind. He seems to have subjected all his religious beliefs to a searching examination and to have applied to them with rigorous logic the standard he found in holy Scripture. His progress was more rapid and definite than that of his great contemporaries Latimer and Cranmer; and he never exhibited the same reluctance to abandon opinions or practices which had nothing to plead in their favour but custom and the practice of the ages.[1]

After the banning of Luther's books at Cambridge, Tyndale withdrew to the country to become the tutor to the children of a Gloucestershire squire. But this, as might be imagined, was unrewarding work for a man of his talents, so he went to London to try to find greater fulfilment in Bishop Tunstal's household. He failed, and went into exile in Germany, where he proceeded straight to the fountain-head at Luther's Wittenberg. Thereafter he spent the rest of his short life in exile, living mainly at Antwerp until his martyrdom in 1536. During the dozen or so years that he spent abroad he was engaged in febrile and unceasing literary activity. In the course of it he produced not only the first English translation of the New Testament in the sixteenth century but also a stream of theological and controversial literature. His career may have been short—shorter than that of most major English reformers—but it was phenomenally productive. Sir Thomas More was surely justified in his description of Tyndale as the "Captain of our English heretics".

Tyndale was not, any more than Luther, primarily a historian. Like the great German, he was to make his most significant and enduring contribution as a translator of the Scriptures and as an expositor of their meaning to his fellow-countrymen. All the same, he possessed a rich and vivid sense of history, especially that of his own country. Almost the only glimpse we have of his childhood is one which gives a graphically illuminating premonition of his lively awareness of his country's past. He recounts in his own words thus:

> Except my memory fail me and that I have forgotten what I read when I was a child, thou shalt find in the English chronicle, how that King Athelstan caused the holy Scripture to be translated into the tongue that then was in England.[2]

This matching interest in an early chronicle and a translation of the Bible into the common tongue could hardly be more characteristic of some of the major concerns of Tyndale's adult life. In all his mature writings it is impossible not to detect his profound awareness of the implications of history. Admittedly only one of his books, *The Practice of Prelates*, has any pretensions to being an historical piece. But the appeal to history, both sacred and profane, and heavy reliance on its authority are unmistakably present at many points in all his writings. The general conclusions which he is at pains to draw from his knowledge of the past are closely parallel to those attributed to some of the earlier Continental reformers in the previous chapter; it would be very strange if they were not. But in any examination of Tyndale's writings there are four characteristic attitudes towards history which may be singled out. They are significant not only in determining Tyndale's own standpoint but also in any assessment of the ways in which the understanding of the past by English Protestant reformers became coloured and conditioned in the sixteenth century. For Tyndale here, as in a number of other important respects, was a most influential and formative pioneer.

First of all, he assigned an extremely important role to the teaching function of scriptural history. A note consistently struck by him is that Scripture contained "first the law, what God commandeth us to do; and secondarily the promises, which God promiseth us again, namely in Christ Jesus our Lord". Then thirdly there were the histories and lives of those to whom God had acted as "a schoolmaster"—a simile dear to many reformers besides Tyndale. These contained "ensamples, first of comfort, how God purgeth all them that submit themselves to walk in his ways, in the purgatory of tribulation, delivering them yet at the latter end, and never suffering any of them to perish that cleave fast to his promises. And, finally, note the examples which are written to fear the flesh, that we sin not; that is, how God suffereth the ungodly and wicked sinners that resist God, and refuse to follow him, to continue in their wickedness; ever waxing worse and worse, until their sin be sore increased and so abominable that if they should longer endure they would corrupt the very elect. But for the elect's sake God sendeth them preachers".[3]

This is a deep-seated and recurrent motif of the value of scriptural history teaching by example. It therefore comes as no surprise to find Tyndale appealing to scriptural precedent over and over again. Not only that, but he carries over into his consideration of other historical episodes, especially those relating to the history of the faith, the same principles of interpretation. So, for instance, in his preface to a work called *The Obedience of a Christian Man* he recalls how, at a number of points in scriptural history, "God, since the beginning of the world, before a general plague, ever sent his true prophets and preachers of the Word to warn the people and gave them time to repent." He cites the example of Noah, Lot, Moses, Aaron, the prophets, and Christ himself. Then he promptly goes on to apply the moral to early British history:

> Unto the old Britons also (which dwelled where our nation doth now) preached Gildas; and rebuked them of their wickedness and prophesied . . . what vengeance would follow except they repented. But they waxed hardhearted; and God sent his plagues and pestilences among them and sent their enemies in upon them on every side and destroyed them utterly.[4]

Having regard to what has already been said under this first heading, it is hardly necessary to labour the second point: that for Tyndale the light by which all history must be read was as the record of God's relationship with whole peoples and also with individual men. No better illustration of this could be found than Tyndale's prologue to his commentary on the Book of Jonah. This particular book of the Old Testament was distinctly popular with the reformers. It was the first book of prophecy which Luther had translated into German. The reasons for the esteem in which it was held are not hard to find. With its dramatic account of God's dealings with a reluctant reformer, and its clarion call to repentance and revival of the true faith, it was very obviously a most appropriate tract for the times. Presenting his translation of the book to his readers, Tyndale characteristically flails his papist opponents for having failed to make effective use of scriptural history to point morals for their own time:

> The lives, stories and gests of men which are contained in the Bible they read as things no more pertaining unto them than a tale of Robin Hood,

whereas on the contrary,

> one of the chiefest and fleshliest studies they have is to magnify the saints above measure and above truth.[5]

This latter was a shrewd and not ill-merited blow at the tendency of the medieval Church to supply all too willingly the fabulous lives of the saints contained in the *Legenda Aurea* and other comparable productions as the staple fare of popular devotion. Tyndale then proceeds to trace the divine retribution which has inescapably followed rejection of God's will: "wheresoever repentance was offered and not received, there God took cruel vengeance immediately", witness the history of Noah's flood, Sodom and Gomorrah, Egypt, the Canaanites, the Israelites, the Jews, the Assyrians, the Babylonians, "and so throughout all the empires of the world". Then, predictably, comes a thrust aimed directly at his own countrymen: a reminder of the fate of those Britons who had failed to heed the warnings of Gildas and of the misfortunes in the shape of civil war and all its evils that befell England in the fifteenth century—not for having deposed its lawful king, Richard II, but for having rejected God's prophet, John Wycliffe. Nor were these mere examples from a dead past. All this had, for Tyndale, a fearful contemporary relevance. God never contracted out of human history:

> And now Christ, to preach repentance, is risen yet once again out of his sepulchre, in which the pope had buried him, and kept him down with his pillars and poleaxes, and all disguisings of hypocrisy, with guile, wiles and

25

falsehood, and with the sword of all princes, which he blinded with his false merchandise. And as I doubt not of the ensamples that are past, so I am sure that great wrath will follow, except repentance turn it back again and cease it.[6]

This notion of the covenant-contract assumed a central place in Tyndale's thinking. "The Old Testament and the New Testament comprised one covenant and a covenant was understood as a contract. God had revealed what men may do and may not do . . . God had bound himself to reward man's obedience, to punish man's disobedience, and to indicate in this life whether a given man stood within or without the covenant." In this way he became the first among English writers to give literary expression to the major theological themes of law, covenant, works and rewards "upon which the Puritan tradition within English-speaking Christianity was built".[7]

The third characteristic to be emphasized is Tyndale's unusually vivid sense of the eternal and unrelenting contest between good and evil, Christ and Anti-Christ. Battle between them had been joined even before history, in the eternal world before the creation and the fall. At a later stage, within history, "Anti-Christ was in the Old Testament and fought with the prophets. He was also in the time of Christ and the apostles . . . Anti-Christ is now and shall endure until the world's end".[8] Tyndale's developing characterization of the nature of Anti-Christ is striking. In his earlier works, in the *Parable of the Wicked Mammon*, just quoted from, he was chiefly concerned to depict it as the power of evil that had always been at work in the world; "not an outward thing, that is to say a man that shall suddenly appear with wonders, as our fathers talked of him. No, verily; for Anti-Christ is a spiritual thing".[9] However, in a later work, *The Obedience of a Christian Man*, Anti-Christ is identified much more closely with the papacy. This concept is still more fully developed in *The Practice of Prelates*. Here Tyndale traced what he regarded as the unlawful seizure of supremacy by Pope Boniface III, a usurpation reinforced by the domination which the popes exercised over the Carolingians and the Holy Roman Empire. In short, "the kingdoms of the earth and the glory of them, which Christ refused, did the devil proffer unto the pope; and he immediately fell from Christ and worshipped the devil". Thereafter, this unholy tyranny of Anti-Christ was maintained by a corrupt priesthood and sycophantic religious orders, by corrupting the Scriptures through false exposition and promoting forgeries like the Donation of Constantine, and by other frauds and dissimulations.[10] Here, of course, Tyndale's exposition is very much in line with that evolved by Continental reformers; but it is none the less noteworthy for its intense and apocalyptic expression.

The fourth characteristic is one that has a particular bearing on the English reformers' interpretation of history. This is the application of Tyndale's exegesis of sacred and profane history to his own country's past. As we saw earlier, from his boyhood upwards he had been deeply attracted to English chronicles. It is patently evident that he retained that interest all his life. In his writings it is possible to trace the origins of four themes which were to be of increasing, ultimately of decisive, consequence in the view of English history adopted by English reformers.

There was first of all his insistence upon the unlawful dominion over the Church of England and also over English kings exercised by the papacy. In his *Practice of Prelates* Tyndale offered what was, at that time, a highly original interpretation of relations between Church and State in medieval England; a vein which was to be intensively exploited by later authors. Reduced to its simplest terms, Tyndale's line was that the history of medieval England was the history of a long and sustained conspiracy on the part of Anti-Christ as represented by the popes and their minions, especially the archbishops of Canterbury, to reduce the kings of England to be their submissive puppets. The object of *The Practice of Prelates* was to show that the actions of men like Anselm, Becket, Stephen Langton, Thomas Arundel or Thomas Wolsey in England were but one ramification of a vast international conspiracy headed by the pope. Its object was to elevate clerical authority and subordinate secular monarchy to it completely. "Howbeit that they (i.e. the prelates) strive among themselves who shall be greatest yet against the temporal power they be always at one."[11] The book ends with a furious onslaught on Thomas Wolsey as the latest, completest and most objectionable embodiment of what was worst in the papacy and its agents. Though in *The Practice of Prelates* Tyndale did no more than give an outline sketch of the idea of the long and continuous plot of the medieval Church against the monarchy it contained all the essentials. Here was the blue-print for the full-scale model later to be built by Bale and especially by Foxe.

Secondly, it inevitably followed from such an interpretation of the role of the medieval papacy that in addition to reducing the secular power to subservience, the spirituality had increasingly corrupted religion. "The wickeder the people are", argued Tyndale, "the more they

27

have these hypocrites in reverence, the more they fear them, and the more they believe in them." In the process of deceiving the laity, he went on, the clergy had not scrupled to "put out God's testament and God's truth, and set up their own traditions and lies, in which they have taught the people to believe, and thereby to sit in their consciences as God".[12] They had, of course, on this showing closed up the Scriptures against the laity so that this unique mirror of truth might not be held up to them and their wickedness revealed. Furthermore, they had falsified or covered up the secular record as well by "putting a great part of the [hi]stories and chronicles out of the way, lest their falsehood should be seen".[13] This last was a more than usually fruitful hint taken up and exploited fully by later reformers: that any searching and critical appeal to the sources of English history, so much corrupted by being for too long the exclusive preserve of monks, would reveal the malignity of the spirituality's influence.

This brings us to the third consideration; that Tyndale himself began the process of seriously revising the history of medieval England in a Protestant sense. What he wanted particularly to argue was that, despite the overwhelming pressure of Anti-Christ and his adherents, more than one attempt had in the past been made to awaken England to her responsibility and peril and to recall her to the path of Christian duty; but all in vain. The early attempts of Gildas to preach repentance to the ancient Britons clearly held a distinct fascination for Tyndale. Well they might, for here was a fervent early reformer who not only inveighed in the grand manner against the shortcomings of contemporary religion but who buttressed all his denunciations with an unfailing wealth of scriptural allusion and justification. Tyndale saw in Gildas a God-sent prophet entrusted with the high task of rebuking his fellow-countrymen for having deserted the Scriptures and followed the vain imaginings of men. Tyndale was no less impressed by condign vengeance which fell upon the ancient Britons for having disregarded the prophet's warnings. But, crucial a series of events as these were, they were very remote in time and little could now be uncovered about them. Much more to Tyndale's purpose were episodes of English history much nearer his own day and generation. We find incidental mention of them scattered at a number of points in Tyndale's writings. Thus in the *Obedience of a Christian Man* he tried to depict King John as an honest ruler trying to do his duty as a king, but being thwarted and humiliated by the papacy. In doing so Tyndale had a double object in view: he not only wanted to revise the long-accepted view of John's relationship with the papacy but he also wanted to show that it was the papacy and the hierarchy who were always the most inveterate enemy and most insubordinate subjects of any ruler. This was in accord with the basic purpose of his book which was to refute the charge brought against the reformers, especially since the outbreak of the Peasants' Revolt in Germany, of being fomenters of rebellion and disorder. But of all Tyndale's reassessments of English history the most significant was his reappraisal of Wycliffe and of the calamitous results for England of the suppression of his doctrine and the persecution of his followers. In his prologue to the commentary on the book of Jonah he contended that

> Wycliffe preached repentance unto our fathers not long since. They repented not; for their hearts were indurate and their eyes blinded with their own pope-holy-righteousness, wherewith they had made their souls gay against the receiving again of the wicked spirit. . . . But what followed? They slew their true and right king, and set up three wrong kings in a row, under which all the noble blood was slain up and half the commons thereto, what in France, and what with their own sword, in fighting among themselves for the Crown; and the cities and towns decayed, and the land brought half into a wilderness, in respect of that it was before.[14]

This was a new, distinctive and highly important slant to the customary explanation for the outbreak of civil wars in fifteenth-century England, that they were brought about by the deposition of the lawful sovereign, Richard II. Tyndale was urging, on the contrary, that that deposition was itself a mere consequence of the rejection of the truth as preached by a great precursor of the Reformation. It was a theme obviously near to his heart and one to which he returned more than once in the prefaces to his scriptural expositions. It was, moreover, one which had unmistakable implications for his own time. The truth had, in his own day, again been revealed and was being preached anew by God's prophets. If it were once more refused and driven out, then all the horrors of fifteenth-century disorder, and perhaps worse, would ensue. "As I doubt not of the ensamples that are past", mused Tyndale gloomily, "so I am sure that great wrath will follow, except repentance turn it back again and cease it."[15]

Finally, closely associated with this deep attraction to the role which Wycliffe and the Lollards had tried to play was Tyndale's conviction that the elect must always be prepared to undergo relentless persecution at the hands of Anti-Christ before truth could ultimately prevail. Forasmuch then, he wrote, as we must needs be baptized in tribulations, and through the Red Sea, and a great and fearful wilderness, and a land of cruel giants, into our natural country; yea and inasmuch as it is a plain earnest that there is no other way into the kingdom of life than through persecution and suffering of pain and of very death, after the ensample of Christ; therefore let us arm our souls with the comfort of Scriptures.[16]

As well as recognizing that persecution must be faced, Tyndale also appreciated the need to maintain an historical record of the sufferings of the persecuted in order to reassure the faithful and strengthen the waverers. He gave practical proof of his concern by himself collecting and publishing the record of the trial of the well-known Lollard, Sir John Oldcastle, and that of William Thorpe. Tyndale was, in his own person, to be one of the earliest and most distinguished English victims of religious persecution in the sixteenth century, did he but know it; and one suspects that he was never long free from apprehension about this, even if he had no actual premonition of it. His own deep concern about the persecution of the elect, his anxiety to preserve and publish some of the records which contained the Wycliffites' teaching and an account of their sufferings, together with his own unhappy fate, were the earliest layers in what was to become an enormous depositum of English martyrology in the sixteenth century. This, as will be seen, was to be one of the most powerful emotive and intellectual forces working in support of reformed religion in sixteenth-century England.

Not one of the others among the first generation of English reformers showed himself to be as historically minded as Tyndale or, in this respect, as interesting in his perceptions. There was, however, one other development of the 1530s which, though no more than indirectly connected with the movement for religious reform, was to prove a powerful ancillary to it. This was the emergence of an eager antiquarian search for books and manuscripts. Its most notable representative in Henry VIII's reign was the King's Antiquary, John Leland. A man of melancholy and unstable personality, Leland evinced a thirst for scholarship that was almost unquenchable. He was profoundly dismayed by the thoughtless dispersal and destruction of the contents of many monastic libraries which accompanied the dissolution of the monasteries. To the task of tracing and preserving all such rare books, manuscripts and source materials he bent all his efforts in the course of his widelyr-anging travels throughout England and Wales. For his pains he is rightly regarded as the founding father of that prolific and energetic swarm of antiquaries, scholars, manuscript collectors and topographers in which Tudor England abounded. He did not publish very much of the fruits of his own researches, but he did initiate a vigorous and lasting tradition. Nor was he himself a very articulate or prominent religious reformer, but his sympathies undoubtedly lay in that direction, and he warmly encouraged other younger men who were of much more enthusiastic—or brasher—religious convictions than he. They seized eagerly upon the sources brought to light by antiquarian scholarship as raw material for belabouring the papacy and extolling reform.

Yet of this first generation it is clearly Tyndale who matters most. It was he, far more than any of his contemporaries, who anticipated some of the most typical and influential concepts and values which Protestant historians in Tudor England would adopt. It must be re-emphasized that he was not primarily a historian nor, apart from *The Practice of Prelates*, were his books historical narratives. He was too much fired by the pressing need to convert his fellow-countrymen in the present to devote much time to the past. Even so, he was historically minded, and he threw out a number of seminal perceptions, hints and suggestions that in some of his successors found a fertile soil in which they throve prodigiously. One of the first and in some ways the most productive of these successors was a man only two or three years younger than Tyndale himself, but one whose development, though not slow, had not been as phenomenally precocious as that of Tyndale. This same man had also been no less powerfully attracted by the antiquarian scholarship of John Leland, one of whose favourite protégés he was. It was that remarkable and inimitable figure among early reformers, John Bale—Bilious Bale.

There can be no doubt that Tyndale's writings left a marked impress on Bale. In one of his most effective early plays, *King John*, there is so close a link between the speeches which Bale put in the mouth of that monarch and what Tyndale had written of him in *The Obedience of a Christian Man* as to suggest that Tyndale's book had been a direct inspiration to Bale. Similarly he was greatly drawn to Tyndale's enthusiasm for the Lollards and his accounts of the persecution they suffered. Bale says in the preface to his own publication of the Examination of Lord Cobham (i.e. Sir John Oldcastle, the Lollard): "I remember that fourteen years ago the true servant of God, William Tyndale, put into the print a certain brief examination of the said Lord Cobham."[17] A little later, Bale repeated with evident approval the suggestion first made by Tyndale of the "wretched calamities" suffered by the realm as the result of the rejection of John Wycliffe's teaching. Another of his early publications which he owed to Tyndale was *The Examination of William Thorpe*. There seems to be no doubt that Bale, like most of his generation of English reformers, was profoundly indebted to Tyndale's writings. And of all this first generation Bale was the one who, by temperament and scholarly interests, was most adequately equipped to develop and intensify that appeal to history which, in Tyndale's works, however pregnant their suggestions, was present only in embryo.

III

THE LINK: JOHN BALE

BALE WAS a near-contemporary of Tyndale, though neither as an author or reformer did he develop with anything like the rapidity of the latter. Bale was born at Cove near Dunwich on November 21, 1495, of not-very-wealthy parents. At an early age he was placed in the Norwich house of the Carmelite friars, a house blessed with a good library, which was from the outset to be a great attraction to Bale. He showed a marked taste for scholarship and soon began to record the history of his own Order. In 1514 he went up to Jesus College, Cambridge, where he was to remain for fifteen years. Among his contemporaries at Cambridge were Thomas Cranmer, Bilney, Latimer, Matthew Parker, Robert Barnes and, for a short space of time, William Tyndale himself. It is not easy now to unravel Bale's friendships and associations at Cambridge, but nearly all those with whom he is known to have had contacts had at least flirted with reforming opinions. Bale himself had by this time very probably been converted to such views, although after leaving the university in 1529 he nevertheless became prior of a number of Carmelite houses.

Having fallen in with Thomas Cromwell's associate, Lord Wentworth, Bale left his own Order and took a wife. He became increasingly active after 1534 in the reforming party, among whom his fluent and provocative pen made him very useful as a propagandist. During this period he wrote a number of plays, all of them with a strong anti-papal slant, and organized his own company of players. In 1536 he got into a certain amount of trouble for his advanced Protestant beliefs. The man who wrote most warmly in his defence to Cromwell was none other than the King's Antiquary, John Leland. Leland, to his credit, spoke up bravely for Bale and testified of him, "Surely if the man be not more strongly changed there is in him learning, judgment, modesty, with many other good qualities."[1] But more to the point in this crisis probably was Cromwell's own regard for Bale. It saved him from harm at this time, and it can hardly be a coincidence that when in 1540 Cromwell fell from power Bale went into exile in various Swiss and

German cities. During the next few years he was engrossed in prolific literary activity and produced a number of books, most of them polemical in character.

He returned to England in 1547 at the accession of Edward VI. For a year or two he was at the household of the duchess of Richmond where he cemented what was to prove a lifelong friendship with the martyrologist, John Foxe, on whom he was to exercise a decisive influence. During the years from 1547 to 1551 Bale appears "vaguely as one of an equally indistinct group of Reformation writers" hanging around the outskirts of the Court.[2] Finally he was elevated to the remote and uninviting bishopric of Ossory in Ireland. His stay there was to be short, vexatious and turbulent. But he showed a hardy courage in publicly maintaining his beliefs, especially after the accession of Mary to the throne. He finally escaped and reached the Continent after an eventful journey on a pirate ship. His short sojourn in Ireland had cost him dear; most grievous of all had been the loss of his splendid private collection of manuscripts. He did not, however, allow this to prevent him from pressing on with his great work of compiling an exhaustive historical catalogue of British authors. During his exile in Basle he was also in close touch with John Foxe and was mainly instrumental in persuading him to proceed with his plans for collecting and publishing material relating to the Protestant martyrs.

When Bale returned to England after Elizabeth's accession to the throne he was a sick and ailing man. For his support he was given a prebend at Canterbury—hardly an adequate reward for one who had shown so signal a constancy to the reforming cause, one would have thought. Ill though he was, Bale's ambition was still to write a new Protestant history of England. In order to achieve this he was desperately anxious to recover that mass of manuscripts of which he had been deprived in Ireland. But, despite the good offices of Matthew Parker, archbishop of Canterbury, he was unable to do so. He died in 1563, with his great project unfulfilled. It was left to his younger friend and protégé, John Foxe, to carry out.

Looking at Bale's life and books, one cannot but be struck by the three-fold inspiration which dominated the whole of them. These three strands can here, for the convenience of analysis, be disentangled; but in Bale's own make-up they were completely and harmoniously interwoven. First, and most readily associated with Bale, was his role as the fiery polemicist and savage critic of the Roman Church. Hardly less well known is that of the antiquary and literary historian; the scholar with the passion for manuscripts and other evidences of the past. And finally there was Bale the fervent English patriot. The primary compulsion of the two last-named sources of inspiration was acknowledged by Bale himself when he declared that what had impelled him to write his most important books were "historiarum dulcedo, literum cupiditas, atque vehementer naturalis et officiosus ergo patriae amor" ("a sweet taste for histories, an eager desire for literature, and an equally strong natural love of my country"). In what follows each of these three characteristic traits is examined more closely to reveal how they found expression in Bale's writings. For our present purpose, it need hardly be added, this analysis will be chiefly concerned with Bale the antiquary and historian.

The first aspect of Bale's writings—the polemical—is well known and has frequently been condemned. It is best summed up in the distasteful epithet "Bilious" so often tacked on to Bale's name. Nor is it undeserved. Bale was anything but mealy mouthed and he never hesitated to draw on an extensive and picturesque repertoire of scurrility and abuse in his attacks on the Roman Church. His modes of expression were as coarse and earthy as any of those employed in that uninhibited and unsqueamish age. In all his comments on his religious opponents he was wholly partisan and bigoted. He would allow his enemies no merit whatever.

In his early plays written in verse, which are of no small interest to students of English literature and drama, the content is undiluted propaganda, and Bale gives free rein to his animus against the papists. One short extract out of any number that might be cited will give a fair example of the unrestrained intensity with which Bale let himself go. In the play, *The Three Laws*, the character called Evangelist attacks Infidelity, False Doctrine and Hypocrisy, all of whom are depicted as pillars of the Roman Church. He says:

> Oh damnable leading of Babylonical sodomites,
> Yourselves ye declare to be shameful hypocrites.
> Lord! Pity thy people and take away these guides,
> These scorners, these robbers, these cruel homicides . . .
>
> Woe, Pharisees, woe! Ye make clean outwardly,
> But inwards ye are full of covetousness and bawdry.
> Painted tombs are ye, appearing right beautiful;
> But within ye stink and have thoughts very shameful.[3]

The extract just quoted could readily be paralleled, both for the indifferent quality of the doggerel and the force of the vituperation, in any of Bale's early morality plays. But the most interesting of these pieces in the present context is the historical play, *King John*. In it Bale was able to do three things in a combination that was peculiarly congenial to him. He was able to unleash his most savage criticism of the papists; he could place it in a historical setting; and he could give it a pressing contemporary relevance. It was a situation which gave him the opportunity of bringing all his gifts and interests into play, and it shows how completely interfused in his own mind, even in his earliest plays, were those three sources of inspiration already referred to. In the play John was depicted as a worthy king, "a faithful Moses", who "withstood proud Pharaoh for his poor Israel". He was not only thwarted in his lifetime by the "blood-suppers" of the clergy but afterwards had his reputation "poisoned" by them "in their malignity", which caused "ill-report of him always to be". "In the desert" England continued to dwell,

> Till that Duke Joshua, which was our late King Henry,
> Clearly brought us into the land of milk and honey.
> As a strong David, at the voice of verity,
> Great Golie, the Pope, he struck down with his sling;
> Restoring again to a Christian liberty
> His land and people, like a most victorious king.[4]

What is possibly even more revealing is that Bale not only denounces the Roman Church for its abuses and for the wrongs it has committed but also for having falsified the record in its own favour. Early on in the play one character called The Nobility says to another called The Clergy:

> It is your fashion such kings to discommend
> As your abuses reform or reprehend.
> You priests are the cause that chronicles doth defame
> So many princes and men of notable name.[5]

Then towards the end of the play, after John's death, Verity says:

> I assure ye, friends, let men write what they will,
> King John was a man both valiant and godly
> What though Polydorus reporteth him very ill
> At the suggestions of the malicious clergy?
> Think you a Roman with the Romans cannot lie?

(This last reference is an illuminating comment on Bale's attitude towards the famous Italian historian, Polydore Vergil, who was engaged on writing a history of England. Bale was too much of a historian not to recognize the Italian's quality in the same field. But as an official of the papal curia Polydore was, in Bale's eyes, too incorrigibly pro-Roman in sympathy ever to have written an acceptable history of England.) Bale therefore ends with a stirring appeal to the pioneer and prince of English antiquaries:

> Yes, therefore, Leland out of thy slumber awake,
> And witness a truth for thine own country's sake!
> For his valiantness many excellent writers make.[6]

Remembering Leland's own notorious tardiness in putting any of his material in print, one cannot help wondering whether Bale was not bracing himself as much as, if not more than, Leland for such an effort. What is certain is that this note that the chronicles and other writings needed to be purified of "Romish lies" so that the history of England might be properly rewritten prefigures the whole tenor of Bale's major efforts throughout his career.

These plays were, of course, early works written when the tension between the king and the pope had reached its pitch. They were undisguisedly a part—and not the least successful one—of the propaganda war then being mounted against papal authority in support of the royal supremacy. It would be idle to look for anything in them but a nakedly one-sided espousal of the anti-Roman line. But this fiercely antagonistic front was, in fact, to be maintained throughout all Bale's writings. Even in his later less polemical work, even in a celebrated work of scholarship like the *Catalogus* of British authors, on which his fame now chiefly rests, it was not absent; and it persisted right to the end of his life. The exceptional acuity of Bale's animus against the papacy was recognized by his contemporaries. One of them, Laurence Humphrey, who was well fitted to judge, maintained that Bale was the Englishman who "most completely tore away the mask that the Pope and popery wore".[7]

We must now turn to the second of Bale's three faces, that of the antiquary and historian. There were a number of other English Protestant authors who castigated the Roman Church with hardly less vigour or abandon than Bale. But there was none who had a comparable equipment or interest to attack it on historical grounds. Of his passionate attachment to historical and literary scholarship and of his genuinely scholarly inclinations and interests there can be no question. He was an antiquary before ever he was a reformer. From his earliest days as a friar he had been an avid student and collector of historical

37

sources. This had, in due course, made him the friend and protégé of John Leland; and Bale regarded it as his mission to continue, expand, and bring to a successful conclusion Leland's task of salvaging the manuscripts of the medieval libraries from the disaster which had engulfed them when the monasteries were dissolved.

However contemptuous Bale may have been of monks, no one could have been more solicitous of their manuscripts. He brought together one of the largest and most comprehensive private collections of anti-quarian manuscripts ever assembled in the sixteenth century. It included nearly all the leading native chroniclers and historians and a large number of foreign authors as well. In all it ran to over 350 items. Probably the completest collection of its kind, it formed the basis of Bale's *Catalogus*, which is still an indispensable work for scholars. The quality and range of Bale's historical scholarship were widely recognized in his own day by great Continental scholars like Matthias Flacius Illyricus and Alesius no less than by his own fellow-countrymen.

Bale was not content with simply collecting, however. He wanted to put his scholarship to what he conceived to be the best uses. He tried to prove that his knowledge of the past confirmed his view of the present, viz., that the papacy was and always had been the tool of Anti-Christ, indeed was the worst manifestation on earth of Anti-Christ himself. The pope and the hierarchy, to secure their hold over Church and State, had monopolized the recording of events and had twisted their account in the interests of their own usurpation and tyranny. Evidence of this attitude has already been cited from his earliest plays. Further confirmation of it is found in another of his earliest works, *The Chronicle of Lord Cobham*, itself a printed attempt to rehabilitate one of the "villains" of monkish propaganda. In this publication Bale flayed Polydore Vergil for "polluting our English Chronicles most shamefully with his Romish lies and other Italian beggaries". He then went on to plead:

> I would wish some learned Englishman to set forth the English Chronicles in their right shape, as certain other lands have done afore them, all affections set apart. I cannot think a more necessary thing to be laboured to the honour of God, beauty of the realm, erudition of the people, and commodity of other lands, next the sacred Scriptures of the Bible, than that work would be.[8]

Taking his own advice to heart, Bale himself made an ambitious attempt to rewrite some aspects of the ecclesiastical history of England and published it in 1546 under the title of *The Acts of English Votaries*.

It is a substantial book of some 400 octavo pages, and it was reprinted in 1548. But no modern edition of it has appeared, and so it has remained largely unknown.

In writing it, Bale was inspired by a number of motives. He wanted to discredit the Roman Church in general. He also wished to "purify" English history of "monkish corruptions" and especially to destroy that image of the English Church popularly enshrined in John Capgrave's very widely known *Catalogus Sanctorum Angliae*, in which the more miraculous versions of English saints' lives were narrated with customary uncritical medieval gusto and exaggeration. Finally, Bale sought to prove that the celibacy of the clergy, far from having raised the level of sanctity in their midst, had in fact grossly and carnally corrupted their morals.

The outline of English church history contained in this book is the first big-scale attempt to give English history a Protestant complexion. As such it is worthy of some attempt at recapitulation. Bale begins with the conversion of Britain, which he places in apostolic times, and attributes it, with marked emphasis, to a *married* man, Joseph of Arimathea, sent over from Gaul by Philip in A.D. 63. Thus, the Britons "took the Christian faith at the very spring or first going forth of the Gospel when the Church was most perfect and had most strength of the Holy Ghost". Established in full apostolic purity, the British Church held fast despite persecution and remained largely uncontaminated until the time of the Anglo-Saxon conquest, when Gregory the Great sent his mission to England headed by Augustine, "not of the order of Christ as was Peter, but of the superstitious sect of Benedict, there to spread abroad the Romish faith and religion, for Christ's faith was there long afore" ... "Well might this be called a new Christianity, for neither was it known of Christ nor of his apostles, nor yet ever seen in England afore. It came altogether from the dust-heap of their monkery." They brought with them all kinds of unscriptural corruptions: "mass offerings, ceremonies, bishops' seats, consecrations, church hallowings, orders giving, tithes, parsonages, purifications of women, and such like". In this fashion did Augustine prepare "Antichrist a seat here in England".[9]

This introduction of popery had equally destructive consequences for the State. It struck a lethal blow at the ancient and glorious empire of the Britons, which came for the first time under nearly a millennium of papal domination. At this point Bale refers to the hoary prophecy of Merlin that the descendants of the ancient Britons would some day be

39

restored to their primeval and rightful position of dominance in the island. But he gives it a particular Protestant twist: that when this restoration came it would mean the freedom of Britain from popish rule. So that for Bale it was not so much the accession of the Tudors as such which had truly fulfilled that prophecy as the assertion of royal supremacy by Henry VIII.

Later personalities associated with the Church in the Saxon period— notably Theodore of Tarsus and Dunstan—far from having reformed the Church, as the English chroniclers had tried to pretend, had only dragged it further down "by sowing of all superstitions, made ready the way to Satan and his filthy kingdom against his coming forth from the bottomless pit, after the full thousand years from Christ's Incarnation".[10] Later, the Norman Anselm, "the great Pope or Antichrist of England",[11] was even more reprehensible, chiefly because he had been primarily responsible for enforcing celibacy, but also because of his opposition to secular power. Throughout the whole book all the miracles and other evidences of holiness customarily attributed to the saints of the Saxon and Norman periods are derided and dismissed as lies or credulity.[12]

Long though the book is, Bale had only half finished it. He took the story down only to A.D. 1200, in two parts, from the conversion of Britain to A.D. 1000, and from 1000 to 1200. However, he gives a clear indication that he had it in mind to proceed to two further instalments, from 1200 to 1400, i.e. from King John to King Henry IV, and from 1400 to 1550. His own summary of his reasons for this periodization reads:

> In the first part, after long engendering, breeding and bringing, my votaries have risen fast, by the crafty inventions of idolaters. In the second part they have builded fast by the witty practices of monks and canons. In the third part shall they hold fast by the busy caulkings of the four orders of friars. And in the fourth part shall they fall fast by the mighty assaults of preachers and writers.[13]

But whatever his ambitions may have been, for some reason or other Bale never fulfilled his plan for completing his history.

In thus recounting the history of the English Church Bale did not, of course, consider it in isolation from the wider course of ecclesiastical history. All the major phases of English history were linked with the history of the papacy itself. One of his best-known books, indeed, was his Latin history of the Popes, *Acta Romanorum Pontificum*, a work of sufficiently wide interest to have been thought worthy of translation into French and German as well as English, in which it is known as *The Pageant of the Popes*. It purports to trace the history of the popes from their origins down to Pope Paul IV (1555-59). Although at first sight it seems to be following the precedent set by Barnes's *Vitae Pontificum*, it is in fact a much more learned, ingenious and subtle onslaught on the papacy than Barnes's pedestrian offering. It is impossible to summarize its contents adequately, but the following outline may give some idea of its author's approach and methods.

The book is divided into three parts. Part I deals with the first and only virtuous phase in the history of the popes, that of the "ancient and holy fathers" from the apostles to Pope Sylvester. These were "godly and faithful pastors, free from all worldly pomp and glory, either in pride of attire, as mitre and pall, or of haughty and ambitious title of Christ's general vicar, but painful preachers of the Gospel, with all humility, and constant martyrs in the end".[14] In Part II came the second sort of popes, the mitred archbishops and patriarchs from Sylvester to Boniface III, who first claimed Roman primacy. Now freed from persecution, these began to grow in wealth and worldly status, "putting rich mitres upon their heads, taking upon them the name of archbishops". "Also they began little by little to add their own devices to God's service . . . and so began to plant and sow in Rome the seed of Antichrist."[15] Part III dealt with the "whole rablement" of popes from Boniface III to Paul IV. This part was further subdivided into five sections designed to show how the history of the papacy accorded with the prophecies contained in the Book of Revelation. Thus from Boniface III to John VIII was the Kingdom of the Great Beast, from John to Sylvester II the Kingdom of the Great Harlot, from Sylvester to Innocent IV the Kingdom of the Dragon, and from Innocent to Julius II the Kingdom of the Locusts. Some idea of the ways in which Bale characterized each of these episodes may be gleaned from the following quotations. Of the Kingdom of the Dragon he wrote:

> Consequently after the thousandth year after Christ's birth, it was prophesied that the devil should be let loose, and this shall be called the Kingdom of the Great Dragon: wherein the acts of the popes do wonderfully answer to it, both in Sylvester II, who with his necromancy raised the Devil from Hell and, having conjured him up, did compound with him for the popedom.[16]

Again, of the Kingdom of the Locusts he wrote:

> for that in this time the Locusts which he interpreteth the new found orders

of begging friars invented and ratified by the . . . popes devour, spoil, waste and destroy all with their sophistical and cavilling doctrine.[17]

As may already have become apparent, this is not an unlearned book and it is in many ways a highly ingenious one. But its tone is violently polemic and it is not serious history in any sense in which we should understand that term. The technique is exactly similar to that which Bale employed in *The Acts of English Votaries*. He seizes upon every moral deficiency and magnifies it out of all proportion. In doing so he shows a somewhat excessive and morbid delight in any sexual delinquency, real or imagined. He is almost equally severe on the political ambitions of the popes and on the avarice and greed which their example had inspired throughout the hierarchy. It need hardly be added that in Bale's opinion it was the popes who were to be blamed for introducing all "superstition", "vain ceremonies", "idolatry", etc., into public worship. Moreover, as with the major figures of the English Church of previous ages so also with the popes, Bale made a frontal attack on any of the great and venerated figures among them, like Gregory I or Gregory VII or Innocent III, and tried utterly to destroy their reputation.

One further very interesting feature that emerges from Bale's *Pageant of the Popes* is its author's concern to establish links between history and prophecy, especially as revealed in that well-spring of scriptural eschatology, the Book of Revelation, which clearly exercised an immense fascination for him. This preoccupation brings out again that deep-rooted conviction of the indissoluble unity of past, present and future in divine plans for mankind which lay at the heart of so much sixteenth-century thinking.

This appears very unmistakably in another of Bale's major works, his *Image of Both Churches*. This has recently been described by a judge as discerning and authoritative as Professor William Haller as Bale's "most clearly conceived and carefully executed work, the one in which the gravity of the subject is most nearly matched by a style free from gross extravagance. The intention of this work was to persuade the English people that the struggle between the believers in the Word and their persecutors was but one more engagement in the age-long contention of Christ and Antichrist described by St John in his Vision".[18] Haller believes that Bale derived his inspiration from Luther or from a Lutheran historian like Matthias Flacius Illyricus. But he could equally well have got it from his fellow-countryman, Tyndale, and it certainly exists in embryo in Bale's early plays. In his preface to the book Bale cites a large number of authors to whom he was indebted, but adds, "Of these commentaries have I taken both example to do this thing and also counsel to understand the text; to none of them wholly addict but as I perceived them always agreeing to the scriptures."[19]

But we need not spend too much time discussing the niceties of Bale's sources of knowledge and inspiration, for the truth is that this concept was a classical Christian one emanating from Eusebius and especially from Augustine's *City of God*, of whom Bale says in his preface: "After the true opinion of St Austin, either we are citizens in the New Jerusalem with Jesus Christ, or else in the old superstitious Babylon with Anti-christ the vicar of Satan."[20]

Many of Bale's modern readers may be much less impressed by this book than Professor Haller appears to be, and may find it distinctly tedious reading. Its contents are not arranged in any historical sequence but consist of a detailed verse-by-verse—one had almost said blow-by-blow—commentary on the Book of Revelation, itself anything but an orderly book. The result is that Bale's comments are inevitably discursive and repetitive, ranging freely from sacred to profane history, from present to past, from past to future, and back again. There are two points of special interest for our present study attaching to this book. The first is that Bale's interpretation of church history is consistent with that given in his more narrowly historical works, that Rome was the "Babylonish whore or disguised synagogue of shavelings", foretold in Revelation and borne out by the evidence of the chronicles.[21] The second is the sense of terrifying relevance which the prophecies of Revelation had for his own time. The horrible persecution of the faithful by the Roman Church was a sure sign that the latter-day judgment was at hand. Bale was convinced of this even in Henry's reign; the vastly intensified persecution of Mary's reign was bound to deepen this conviction still more steadfastly. It also led him on to believe that England had a role of special responsibility in the divine ordering of terrestrial history. This brings us to the third characteristic of Bale which we wish particularly to discuss—his fervent patriotism.

Bale's was a particular kind of patriotism, of course. He took that xenophobia and dislike of foreigners so widespread in Henry VIII's England and gave it a distinctively Protestant and anti-papal cast. In all his studies of the English past Bale eagerly seized upon every episode, every event, every personality that might illumine and confirm his thesis of a manifest destiny for his country. Above all he wanted to reinforce the notion of a continuing golden thread, a genuine apostolic succession of true believers from Joseph of Arimathea's first converts onwards. This he believed to have been maintained by the despised and neglected genuine Christian martyrs, "the preachers of the gospel, or poor teachers hereof in corners, when the persecution was such that it might not be taught abroad. And these poor souls, or true servants of God, were put to death by the holy spiritual fathers, bishops, priests, monks, canons and friars".

Between such true martyrs and the pseudo-martyrs of the Roman persuasion Bale drew a crucial distinction. The papist pseudo-martyrs were "monastery-builders and chantry-founders whom the temporal princes and secular magistrates have diversely done to death, sometime for disobedience and sometime for manifest treason".[22] Among the true martyrs he held none in greater esteem than the followers of Wycliffe. Bale, following Tyndale, had a special regard for the Lollards. Wycliffe he recognized as a pioneer and precursor of outstanding significance. Here was a "true servant of Jesus Christ, a man of very excellent life and learning", who "for the space of more than twenty-six years most valiantly battled with the great Antichrist of Europe, or pope of Rome, and his diversely disguised host of anointed hypocrites to restore the Church again to that pure estate that Christ left her in at his ascension".[23]

Nothing was more satisfying to Bale's instincts as Protestant, patriot and book-collector than to search for all of Wycliffe's scattered writings and those of his Lollard followers. Bale claimed to have in his own possession no fewer than 144 of these works,[24] and he also wrote two books in defence of Wycliffe. The close connexion between Lollard survivals and the early Protestant reformers of Tudor England and the high esteem placed by the latter on the writings of the Lollards are subjects to which scholars have rightly drawn much attention in recent years. Among the early Protestants no one was better versed in Lollard literature than Bale, or more influential in making known among his co-religionists this distinctive English contribution to the reform of the Church. He was equally anxious to give publicity to those documents relating to the trial and condemnation of what he described as those "godly and valiant warriors, which have not spared to bestow their most dear lives for the verity of Jesus Christ against the malignant muster of that execrable Antichrist of Rome, the devil's own vicar".[25] Like Tyndale he published an account of Oldcastle and Thorpe. He later added to this the history of the trial and execution of Mistress Anne Askew.

Most far-reaching of all was his influence on John Foxe. No one did more than Bale to convince Foxe of the absolute necessity of putting on record the sufferings of the faithful, without which the true Church could never be born: "She is pained with labours, dolours, blasphemies, troubles and persecutions, and never is delivered without them. Never is Christ earnestly received till some of her members do suffer."[26]

The full fall-out of the influence of Bale's view of British history did not come until the Elizabethan Age. It made a considerable impact on the chroniclers of secular history like Hall and Holinshed who accepted his interpretations when dealing with controversial figures like Old-castle for example. Still more stimulating was his influence on Arch-bishop Parker and other antiquaries, partly as a scholar, even more as a collector of manuscripts. But the man who was most truly his spiritual heir was John Foxe, whose *Book of Martyrs* was to be the consummation of all that Bale had most devoutly wished.

IV

THE CONSUMMATION: JOHN FOXE

MUCH, THOUGH NOT ALL, of the flowering of Protestant historiography so far discussed took place during the reigns of Henry VIII and Edward VI. The chill winds of Marian reaction, as might have been expected, checked its growth. Yet despite the adversities of Mary's reign, interest in Protestant historiography was far from being extinguished. Amid the groups of English reformers in exile on the Continent strenuous efforts were made to maintain a sturdy output of appropriate scholarship and literature. Some directed their energies to outbursts of politicoreligious propaganda. Others were chiefly occupied with the Genevan Bible—without doubt the most far-reaching single achievement on the part of the exiles.

There was another group engaged in recording Protestant history, especially a chronicle of the sufferings of the martyrs in England. The three men most closely associated with this martyrology were John Bale, John Foxe and Edmund Grindal, later to be bishop of London and archbishop of Canterbury. In 1555 Grindal, from exile, was maintaining close touch with the leading reformers imprisoned at home. Once it had become unmistakable that an all-out policy of persecution had been embarked upon, Grindal pushed ahead with his plans for a history of the martyrs' sufferings.[1] But overshadowing Grindal himself in this venture were his two collaborators, Bale and Foxe. The former had long held the strongest views on the need for such a compilation. The latter was to execute with supreme success the whole design for a large-scale Protestant martyrology.

Before the exiles' sojourn on the continent was unduly protracted, however, Mary died in November 1558. The exiles now returned— "the wolves came back from Geneva", to quote one unflattering contemporary papist comment—to occupy a place of some importance in the religious life of Elizabethan England. They were in a key position to establish a reformed ideology, and not the least essential component of it was their Protestant view of history. The whole notion of the

46

particular nature of British history was assiduously fostered in book, sermon and scholarship.

The primate of the Church himself gave a powerful lead. Matthew Parker, archbishop of Canterbury, though not himself an exile, was much in sympathy with the views of many of his suffragans who had been. He was deeply absorbed in questions concerning the early history of the Church in Britain and vitally concerned to prove its proto-Protestant antecedents.[2] During his years of office as archbishop, despite the many preoccupations of his political and ecclesiastical responsibilities, Parker industriously explored any clues that might lead him to books and manuscripts which could shed light on early British church history. To this end he exploited his official position and got the Privy Council to agree to his having a "special care and oversight" for "such ancient records and monuments".[3] He maintained about him a body of scholars and experts and a team of highly skilled craftsmen to deal with his books and manuscripts, of which he became an outstanding collector.

Nor was he content merely to collect. True to his ambition of extending widely a knowledge of early church history, he was "more than any other man responsible for publishing the sources of English history. He either himself edited, or at least supervised the editing of, a long series of texts nearly all printed for the first time".[4] His own most important publication was the *De Antiquitate*, which represents the consummation of his labours as a scholar and a searcher-out of sources. A handsome folio volume of more than 400 pages, it gave in its introductory section an outline history of the British Church before the coming of Augustine. Its emphasis was particularly that Britain was converted directly by the Apostles and not from Rome, and that Christianity was firmly established in the island long before Gregory the Great ever sent his mission.

With a man of Parker's outlook and interest at the head of the hierarchy it was hardly surprising that the Protestant view of church history should become regarded as part of the official doctrine of the English Church. In the writings of its most celebrated early Elizabethan apologist, John Jewel, there is clear evidence of it, especially in his voluminous *Defence* of the *Apology*.[5] Nor was this general line seriously disturbed by controversies between those who upheld the Elizabethan establishment and their Puritan critics. Thomas Cartwright, for instance, might be very severe on some of Whitgift's expositions of early church history. But, far from wanting to impugn the general validity of the Protestant interpretation, Cartwright wanted to take it a stage further by dismissing entirely the whole of Geoffrey of Monmouth's account of the Lucius-Eleutherius relationship, with its dangerous implications of papal intervention and a royally founded episcopate—the latter hardly less obnoxious than the former to an earnest Puritan.[6]

But of all those who, in Elizabeth's realm, were engaged in the study and writing of church history, there was one whose importance far transcended that of all others. Whereas in the writings of almost all other Elizabethan authors on the subject these themes constituted no more than scattered references and tentative outlines, in the pages of one contemporary of genius they were brought together on an epic scale in an ambitious, coherent and not inartistic whole. Linked there in thematic unity with the most exciting as well as the most detailed history of the progress of the Reformation in sixteenth-century England, they gained a power and significance which made them an instinctive motif of English religious thought and emotion, patriotism and history, for centuries.

The author of this spellbinding work was John Foxe. His *Book of Martyrs* has long been recognized as one of the most formative books in the history of the English-speaking peoples. After the Bible it ranks with *Pilgrim's Progress* as the most powerful shaper of English religious attitudes and values. For centuries it found a place of honour on the bookshelf of almost every home where English books, however few in number, were read and treasured. Its dog-eared pages and thumb-grimed woodcuts provided edification and diversion for generations of readers.

But for close on a century Foxe's reputation suffered a somewhat ignominious eclipse in many quarters. The distaste of Tractarian and High Church critics for a work so unblushingly Puritan and Low Church in tone; the criticisms of historians becoming accustomed to a much higher standard of impartiality; and the decline in the authority of revealed religion; all these considerations contributed to a tendency to dismiss the *Book of Martyrs* as an unbridled outburst of partisan propaganda, uncritical and misleading, of negligible value, viewed historically or morally.

However, in more recent times Foxe's merits and reliability as a historian have once again come more into their own. No one would, of course, try to deny his intense partisanship; but there is much to be said for him, as we shall see, as an incredibly industrious and surprisingly accurate searcher out and transcriber of original materials. Even more

48

to the point is the memorable book recently published by the *doyen* of American students of Puritan life and letters, Professor William Haller, who has brought out so brilliantly that, whatever Foxe's latter-day critics may have thought of him as an historian, his contemporaries and many successive generations regarded his book as being second only to the Scriptures as a true and necessary record of God's ways to men. Few of these Englishmen, doubtless, actually knew of Luther's maxim that "history and Scripture entirely coincide"; but in spirit they would certainly have agreed that as far as their own country was concerned Foxe's writing was the completest vindication of such an assertion.

The life-story of the man who came to write a book religiously radioactive for so long can be summarized very briefly. A native of Boston in Lincolnshire and born about the year 1517, Foxe had been educated at Brasenose and Magdalen Colleges, Oxford. He became a Fellow of Magdalen but, being suspected of Protestant sympathies, he gave up his fellowship to become a country vicar for a time. Later, after a short spell as a tutor to the Lucy family's children at Charlecote, he entered the household of the widowed duchess of Richmond in the same capacity. Here he met, became very close friends with, and was powerfully influenced by, John Bale.

In the spring of 1554 he went abroad into exile, first to Strasbourg, later to Frankfort, and finally to Basle, where he was again closely associated with Bale and Grindal. In exile he was assiduously collecting material for the first edition of the work that was later to become his *Book of Martyrs*. This was published in Latin in 1554 under the title *Commentarii rerum in ecclesia gestarum; maximarumque, per totam Europam, persecutionum, a Vvicleui temporibus ad hanc usque aetatem descriptio*.

Back home again from exile, in Elizabethan London he devoted himself with dedicated single-mindedness to enlarging and improving the book which was to be his life's work. In 1563 he published the first English version running to some 1,800 pages, and met with immediate success. A greatly enlarged edition was published in 1570 in two very large volumes; and the last edition to be published in Foxe's lifetime appeared in 1583, also in two volumes. The first of the two volumes published in 1570 contained many important additions, most notably a history of the English Church from the first conversion of the ancient Britons down to Henry VIII's reign.

This was the first real attempt to rewrite the ecclesiastical history of England on a full scale. It was the ambition which Bale had always set himself, but which he had only very partially achieved in either the

Catalogus or, more especially, *The Acts of the English Votaries.* In the latter he had not got beyond 1200; moreover, the book had, in any event, set itself the negative task of pulling to pieces the traditional medieval view of the history rather than the positive statement of the Protestant interpretation. As long as Bale had lived in hopes of fulfilling his dearest project, his friend Foxe was unlikely to have embarked on such a scheme. It may well have been Bale's death in 1563, with his plans not even properly begun, that inspired Foxe to attempt the task of prefacing his account of the more recent events in England with a long account of earlier British church history. He would also, by this time, have been likely to derive greatly added help and inspiration from the labours of Archbishop Parker, who was his chief patron, and other similarly minded scholars.

It goes virtually without saying that Foxe was deep in debt to the example and inspiration of earlier authors. The precedent of scriptural history in Old Testament and New exercised a compelling authority over him. In his dedicatory epistle to the Queen he pointed the moral that "as we see what light and profit cometh to the Church by histories in old times set forth, of the Judges, Kings, Maccabees, and the Acts of the Apostles after Christ's time; so likewise may it redound to no small use in the Church, to know the acts of Christ's martyrs now, since the time of the apostles".[7]

The themes of some of the early patristic authors, too, and especially those of Eusebius, had laid him captive. It was not just that in the earliest sections of his book, where he described the sufferings of the first Christian martyrs, Foxe leaned heavily on Eusebius's authority. It was Eusebius's whole keynote that was uniquely attuned to Foxe's vision of his own time: that Christian truth could only be maintained whole and undefiled by the steadfastness of the elect in the teeth of all the fury of persecution by the ungodly; that triumph must be born of suffering. Foxe was at one with the "father of ecclesiastical history" in his determination to "provide not only the historical record but the lessons to be drawn from it".[8] And he was no less certain than Eusebius had been that he, too, must record "those *peaceful* wars, fought for the very peace of the soul, and men who in such wars have fought manfully for truth rather than for country, for true religion rather than for their dear ones, that my account of God's commonwealth will inscribe on imperishable monuments".[9]

But overriding all else was Foxe's conviction that his latter-day martyrs had as essential a battle-order in the grand strategy of the

Church Militant against the hosts of Antichrist as those early victims described by Eusebius had had.

> If martyrs are to be compared with martyrs, argued Foxe, I see no cause why the martyrs of our time deserve any less commendation than the others in the primitive church; which assuredly are inferior to them in no point of praise, whether we view the number of them that suffered, or the greatness of their torments, or their constancy in dying, or also consider the fruit that they brought, to the amendment of posterity, and the increase of the gospel. They did water with their blood the truth that was newly springing up; so these, by their deaths, restored it again, being sore decayed and fallen down. . . . Seeing we have found so famous martyrs in this our age, let us not fail them in publishing and setting forth their doings; lest in that point, we seem more unkind to them than the writers of the primitive church were unto theirs.[10]

There were other sources of inspiration nearer in time to Foxe. For nearly half a century reformers had been assaulting the papacy and challenging, at many points and from a variety of angles, its version of Christian history. In Germany, by the time that Foxe was writing, this harvest of criticism and reappraisal had ripened into the grandiose re-writing of the history of the Christian Church according to the reformers' vision of the truth at the hands of Flacius and the Centuriators of Magdeburg. At home in England, Tyndale, Bale and others had charted the paths which a Protestant historiography might take.

The most fruitful single influence of the many brought to bear on Foxe was undoubtedly that of Bale. The younger man owed much to his older friend. The broad-sweeping apocalyptic view of the great phases of Christian history and how the machinations of Antichrist fitted into it; the image of the two churches, the one the false church of Rome and the other "the poor oppressed and persecuted church of Christ"; the insistence on the need drastically to revise the accepted view of Christian and secular history, based all too slavishly on that opaque and distorting mirror which monkish chroniclers had held up to events; the peculiarly English emphasis on recent history with reference to the place of Wycliffe, the Lollards and the martyrs since 1400; all these things and much else Foxe had learnt to a large extent at Bale's feet.

The recent development of English history itself was a further motive force of compelling urgency. The Marian reaction had bitten deep and had shown how precarious the hold of reformed religion might be; while the gains of the Counter-Reformation on the Continent were an alarming spectacle. So much seemed once more to depend on England as the home of true religion. More than ever she seemed called forth to a splendid but hazardous manifest destiny as the cradle and champion of reform. But it could be fulfilled, in the eyes of convinced reformers, only as long as the Queen's subjects were perfectly clear about what the course of events in their country's history, distant and near, portended.

But Foxe's *Book of Martyrs* is much more than the sum of the influences brought to bear on its author. Whatever he may have owed to his English friends and mentors he far outstripped them in the scale and influence of his own writing. He was a man of rare and original gifts whose quality we should not lightly underestimate. That he was *parti pris* we need no reminding; but then so were all the writers of his age. That he had talents as a scholar and writer far in advance of many of his contemporaries needs an emphasis greater than it usually receives. There are a number of features of Foxe's book which should still command a modern historian's respect and interest. They make him not unworthy to be ranked among the great English historians.

First, there is the sheer scale of the work. It becomes necessary to mention this because not many people are nowadays familiar with the *Book of Martyrs* at all, and those who do have some nodding acquaintance with it know it only from abridgements. It may be as well to remind ourselves that the edition published by Foxe in 1570 consisted of two large folio volumes running to more than two thousand pages between them, and that one of the standard editions of the nineteenth century runs to some eight volumes of several hundred pages each. The first half of this monumental book runs from the beginnings of the Christian Church to the reign of Henry VIII and the second covers in great depth the history of England from Henry's reign to that of the early years of Elizabeth. The whole work is documented in immense detail, many of the sources in the second half having been published for the first time by Foxe and not a few of them being found in print only in his book still.

Again, the range and variety of the sources which Foxe used, and his technique in relation to them, call for comment. He went far beyond the printed books with which most of his contemporaries contented themselves. Partly this was because he shared the now familiar and inevitable Protestant suspicion of corrupt monkish sources. These chroniclers, he alleged, "taking upon them to intermeddle with matters of the church, although in part they express some truth in matters concerning the bishops and see of Rome, yet in suppressing another part, they play with us, as Ananias and Sapphira did with their money, or as Apelles did in Pliny, who, painting the one half of Venus coming out of the sea, left the other half imperfect: so these writers, while they show us one half of the bishop of Rome, the other half of him they leave imperfect and utterly untold".[11]

But, prejudice apart, Foxe was not lacking a measure of healthy scholarly scepticism for an untrustworthy historical source. Of Arthur's great "'victories and conquests not only over this land but also over all Europe", as chronicled by Geoffrey of Monmouth, he offered this shrewd assessment: "I judge them more fabulous than that any credit should be given unto them; and more worthy to be joined with the Iliads of Homer than to have place in any ecclesiastical history."[12] What is chiefly to Foxe's credit, however, is his insistence upon the need to get at the original sources themselves. In the course of a bout of verbal fisticuffs with his Catholic critic, "Alan Cope" (i.e. Nicholas Harpsfield, the Marian archdeacon of St. Paul's), Foxe emphasized with genuine historian's instinct "it is not sufficient to see what 'Fabian' or what 'Hall' saith; but the records must be sought, the registers must be turned over, letters also and ancient instruments ought to be perused, and authors with the same compared; finally, the writers amongst themselves one to be conferred with another; and so with judgment matters are to be weighed; with diligence to be laboured; and with simplicity, pure from all addition and partiality, to be uttered".[13] A refreshingly modern approach in a sixteenth-century author, and advice by no means inappropriate to the historian today.

These precepts were based on Foxe's own practice. He had himself burrowed near and far among unpublished sources for materials; not merely among the chroniclers but also among letters, charters, episcopal records and registers, and any other manuscript sources which contained material relevant to his purpose, not to mention his extensive use of the oral evidence of eye-witnesses of recent martyrdoms. His transcripts of such material, where they can now be checked, are in general full and accurate.

Another remarkable and praiseworthy feature of Foxe's book is the way in which he quoted *in extenso* the sources on which his account was based. This he did even when they were hostile to all his sympathies and convictions. In his very long and fully documented accounts of Becket or Huss, for example, he cites papal material in support of the former and in condemnation of the latter. In these respects he shows a surprising modernity in his search for and provision of the basic sources.

One of the features of Foxe's book which took the firmest hold of his contemporaries' imagination was the expansive panorama of the whole history of Christendom which it unfolded. Though his earliest and chief concern had been, and remained, the recent history of the church of England he had, by the notable additions of the 1570 version, placed it within a universal perspective of that history of Christianity in Europe and England from apostolic times of which it was an integral part. Such a procedure, far from blurring the edges of the English story or diminishing its distinction, gave it enhanced worth and meaning. In his overall periodization of the history of the Church, Foxe saw it as having passed through five ages of some three hundred years each since the life and death of its founder. These he characterized, at the outset of his book, as follows.

First, there had come the "suffering time" of the Church which lasted for three hundred years until the reign of Constantine. Then came three hundred years of "flourishing time" until the first rise of the papacy at the time of Pope Boniface and the Emperor Phocas. This was followed by three centuries of "declining or backsliding" until the "loosing out of Satan, which was about the thousandth year after the nativity of Christ". "Fourthly, followed the time of Antichrist . . . in which time both doctrine and sincerity of life were utterly, almost, extinguished . . . through the means of the Roman bishops, especially counting from Gregory VII called Hildebrand, Innocent III, and the friars which with him crept in, till the time of John Wickliff and John Huss." Finally, there had come "the reformation and purging of the Church of God, wherein Antichrist beginneth to be revealed".[14]

This scheme appeared to be clear-cut and plausible enough. At a later stage in his book, however, Foxe fell into some confusion and inconsistency. This arose out of his seeming change of mind about when Satan had first been bound in his thousand years of captivity as recorded in the Book of Revelation. If this had taken place in Christ's lifetime, then the loosing of Satan had occurred c. A.D. 1000 and must have coincided with the beginnings of the rapid exaltation of papal power in the eleventh century. This was what Foxe appeared to have originally accepted. But such an interpretation was difficult to square with the persecutions and martyrdoms of the first three hundred years of church history. The ending of such oppression of the godly must surely have been the point at which Satan was bound. This being so, it must have coincided with the establishing of the authority and dominion of the Church by Constantine. In that event, it followed that the second loosing out of Satan must have taken place in the fourteenth century and must have been heralded by a fresh outbreak of persecution. This was the revised explanation which Foxe appeared to have super-imposed on his original thesis in an elaborate introduction to Book VI of his work.[15] But whichever way these events were interpreted England retained her place of honour. For it was one of her sons, John Wycliffe, who "in these so great and troublous times and horrible darkness of ignorance, what time there seemed in a manner to be not one so little a spark of pure doctrine remaining . . . by God's providence sprang and rose up, through whom the Lord would first waken and raise up the world again".[16]

The ingenuities of these eschatological speculations, however deeply they moved and fascinated Foxe and his contemporaries, are apt to leave the modern reader cold. But whatever their shortcomings in modern eyes, they must at least be credited with having stimulated Foxe into directing his readers' attention to the wider horizons of European history.

As might be expected, he portrays at some length decisive changes in the nature of the papacy: "Forsomuch as the church of Rome in all these ages . . . hath challenged to itself the supreme title and ringleading of the whole universal church on earth . . . in writing, therefore, of the Church of Christ, I cannot but partly also intermeddle with the acts and proceedings of the same Church, forsomuch as the doings and orderings of all other churches from time to time, as well here in England as in all other nations, have this long season chiefly depended on the same."[17]

Similarly he traces in some detail the history of Islam which he saw as a parallel strand with the rise of the papacy in the growing challenge of Antichrist. For it was no coincidence in the eyes of Foxe or other reforming historians that the origins of Islam should be traceable to the early seventh century, that is to say at the very time when the papacy was arrogating to itself its usurped and tyrannical authority over Christendom; or again that from the mid-fourteenth century onwards, when Satan was loose again, when Rome was intensifying its campaign of persecution against Wycliffe, Huss, and other rebels against its régime, these things should be accompanied in eastern Europe by the rise of the most recent and most terrifying of all Islamic states, the empire of the Ottoman Turks.

In his treatment of the European scene Foxe was deeply anxious to direct his readers' notice to the image of the other church, the "poor oppressed and persecuted church of Christ", as he called it. This he found among the persecuted minorities, the suppressed and martyred precursors of reform, whom medieval historians had depicted only as subversive and dangerous heretics. Not that their true nature was easy to discover, even for the sympathetic historian. This was because medieval historians, confronted with any who had presumed to oppose the "pope, or his papal pride, or withstand and gainsay his beggarly traditions, rites and religions, . . . in writing of them do, for the most part, so deprave and misreport them . . . that they make them and paint them forth to be worse than Turks and infidels".[18] Such were the Waldensians of the twelfth century or the Albigensians of the thirteenth, for whom Foxe did his best with the scanty materials at his disposal. When it came to Wycliffe and the Lollards, of course, he was in a position to give them more or less full treatment. The links between Wycliffe and Huss, and between Huss and Luther, were expounded *in extenso*. Mention of Luther serves as a reminder that Foxe was the first English historian to give a serious and detailed account of the great German reformer. So it would be not unfair to say that there was nothing narrow or insular in the perspective which Foxe was offering his readers.

Even so, it was the island of Britain that really claimed Foxe's attention. "I have proposed," he informed his readers, "principally to tarry upon such historical acts and records as most appertain to this my country of England and Scotland."[19] And it was this which offered him scope for his most formidable qualities. Like Eusebius, he explicitly disclaimed any intention of dwelling overlong on military or political history—for this he referred his readers to the secular chroniclers. Yet in fact, because the Church bulked so large in the earlier history of Britain and because of the many conflicts between State and Church, Foxe had perforce to cast his net much wider than amid the ecclesiastical shoals only. Overall, indeed, he provided his readers with a pretty solid framework of general English history. But the task to which everything else was subordinated was that full-scale rewriting of English church history along Protestant lines which had been steadily in the making ever since Tyndale's day.

Here was that "learned Englishman" whom Bale and others had wished to see "setting forth the English chronicles in their right shape". This was the record being freed from "monkish fantasies". Now the unique English story as the reformers saw it had been set in their context of the cosmic drama of eternal conflict between the powers of light and darkness. Partisan? Yes, indeed. Biased? Undoubtedly. But, in the eyes of those who believed in it, an unrivalled theme of epic proportions. And one to which Foxe rose magnificently.

It would take far too long to pursue him through all the stages of his history. One can do no more than take one or two typical examples to illustrate his general approach. Let us take one instance, which admirably typifies his method, from a very early period. This is his treatment of that celebrated Lucius-Eleutherius relationship. It was characteristic of Foxe—and it is a virtue not often allowed him by his critics—that he should publish in full the text, as it was available to him, of the supposed letter from Eleutherius to Lucius, even though in some respects it might appear to be very damaging to the Protestant view of what relations between a king and a pope ought to be. Equally, it was no less typical of Foxe that he should emphasize that "after this manner . . . was the Christian faith first brought in, or else confirmed, in this island of Britain by the sending of Eleutherius, not with any cross or procession, but only at the simple preaching of Fagan and Damian". Just as inescapable a part of Foxe, too, was it that he should go on to point an urgent contemporary moral: that Lucius the Christian king died without issue, and as a result "such trouble and variance fell among the Britons (as it happeneth in all other realms, and namely in this realm of England, whensoever succession lacketh), that not only they brought upon them the idolatrous Romans, and at length the Saxons, but also enwrapped themselves in such misery and desolation".[20] There was a clear and uncompromising message here for the Queen and her subjects.

Again, coming down to the Middle Ages, we may contrast his portrayal of that hero of medieval chroniclers, Anselm, with what he says of Wycliffe, whose heresy chroniclers were hard put to find words harsh enough to condemn. In each instance Foxe quoted liberally from the original sources, but of Anselm, archetype of the medieval cleric whose standpoint and values were most abhorrent to him, he wrote:

Thus have ye heard the tedious treatise of the life and doings of Anselm, how superstitious in his religion, how stubborn against his prince he was, what occasion of war and discord he would have ministered by his complaints . . . what zeal without right knowledge what fervency without cause he pretended, what pains without profit he took; who, if he had bestowed that time and travel in preaching Christ at home to his flock, which he took in gadding to Rome to complain of his country, in my mind, he had been better occupied.[21]

In passing, we might note that as a fair example of Foxe's admirably direct, vigorous and sinewy English prose, of which he was a much greater master than is commonly recognized.

So much for Anselm; in sharp contrast are his views on Wycliffe. Of that very harbinger, in Foxe's eyes, of the second dawn of the gospel, his praise, though lavish, was by no means uncritical.

> Through God's providence, he claimed, there stepped forth into the arena that valiant champion of the truth, John Wickliff; whom the Lord, with the like zeal and power of spirit, raised up here in England, to detect more fully and amply the poison of the pope's doctrines, and the false religion set up by the friars. In whose opinions and assertions, albeit some blemishes perhaps may be noted; yet such blemishes they be, which rather declare him to be a man that might err, than who directly did fight against Christ our Saviour, as the pope's proceedings and those of the friars did.[22]

Yet whatever may be the interest and merit of Foxe's account of the earlier history of England, not even the most blinkered pedant could fail to recognize that the real motive power of his work for him, his contemporaries, and subsequent generations was his narrative of his own times. Over a thousand years before Foxe, the greatest of Christian martyrologists had pleaded "it is surely a matter of the highest importance that for the enlightenment of future generations I should set down the events of my own day, calling as they do for a most careful record".[23] Foxe was no less conscious of a comparably onerous responsibility resting on him. Having professed the becoming modesty about his talents expected of a sixteenth-century author, he none the less decided,

> when I weighed with myself what memorable acts and famous doings this latter age of the Church hath ministered unto us by the patient sufferings of the worthy martyrs, I thought it not to be neglected that so precious monuments of so many matters, meet to be recorded and registered in books, should lie buried by my default, under darkness of oblivion. . . . Nothing did so much stir me forward hereunto as the diligent consideration and special regard of the common utility which every man plentifully may receive by the reading of these our "monuments" or martyrology.[24]

His account of the five years of Mary's reign took up nearly half the space of his very bulky book. It is what has always given his work its unique flavour and particularity, and continues to do so. Without it the rest of Foxe's history, however interesting and valuable as a framework, would quickly have vanished into antiquarian limbo. What gave the *Book of Martyrs* its staying-power was the overwhelming force and immediacy of its presentation of the most fateful choice which Tudor England had had to make. In recognizing what was at stake Foxe was not alone. Many of his fellow-countrymen were, like him, intuitively aware, with widely varying degrees of clarity, that the prime politico-religious issue of the age, fought out in England with gathering momentum from Henry VIII's reign onwards, had reached its culmination in Mary's reign.

But Foxe it was, more than any other man, who invested that trial of strength with a drama and anguish of Old-Testament starkness that raised it to a plane of larger-than-life decision. It was he who triumphantly imposed his vision of Mary's reign as the fiery furnace from which God's new chosen people had emerged victorious. A self-satisfying blend of national pride and religious conviction had already proved irresistible in its appeal to Tudor Englishmen. In the *Book of Martyrs* it reached its apogee. A "white legend", as well as a black, incalculably potent and enduring, had been created.

Much of Foxe's narrative is by modern standards admittedly prosy, tedious and weighed down with a daunting ballast of interminable verbatim quotation of source-material. Some of it must have made slow reading for even those earnest-minded men of Tudor and Stuart times whose appetite for prolix, didactic edification was well-nigh boundless. But this should not blind us to its many skilful and appealing traits. Not the least of these was that its readers had ample scope for self-identification with that army of Marian victims. The martyrs were a remarkable cross-section of English society; drawn alike from lay and cleric, old and young, male and female, rich and poor, learned and simple. Their story, steeped in pious hagiographical detail, was often told in their own words. The impact of this sort of auto-recital, as Professor Haller reminds us, had exciting and far-reaching consequences. "The intoxication of these people with the sound of their own voices speaking all manner of things in their own language would in the next generation break out in poetry and drama as well as in martyr tales and sermons, in parliament and the press as well as in the pulpit."[25]

Foxe's account of the sufferings of the martyrs played upon the whole gamut of his readers' emotions from horror and indignation through to admiration and pity. He himself had a sensibility to suffering and a revulsion against its wanton infliction rare to the point almost of being unique in his age. He was minded, he confessed,

somewhat to expostulate with the cruelty of the world. Forasmuch as all mankind having put apart all use of humanity have so far degenerated even unto the iron age, or rather unto a brutal cruelty, that never, as I think, since the beginning of the world was Plautus's proverb more verified, "one man is a wolf unto another"; but amongst the wolves they are most cruel which are clothed in lambs' skins, which also so most profess peace.[26]

(This horror at the cruelties of persecution so manifest in all Foxe's writing was far from being equally characteristic of his readers in his own and subsequent generations.)

Hatred of cruelty did not mean that Foxe was anything but completely committed to his own point of view. He would have conceived of any attempt to present the papal standpoint as being at best a weakness, at worst a breach of the most sacred trust. Even so, compared with many authors among his co-religionists, notably his mentor, John Bale, Foxe was much more restrained, much more willing to quote the evidence. To paraphrase a later editorial maxim, facts—or at least documents—were in general sacred to him, though his comment on them might be very free. Nor was he anything like as savagely vituperative as many of his fellows. For example, his treatment of that much-hated monk, Augustine of Canterbury, the man execrated by Protestants as being responsible for having first soiled with Roman degradation a British Church hitherto unsullied, though by no stretch of the imagination sympathetic, is incomparably less biased and slanderous than that given by Bale. And sternly though Foxe might upbraid Mary for being a "vehement adversary and persecutor against the sincere professors of Christ Jesus and his gospel", his final summing-up of her public calamities and her private misfortunes is not without its notes of genuine compassion for her "unlucky and rueful reign".[27]

And yet, of course, it was because Foxe was so *engagé*, because he believed so utterly in the rightness of his cause, and the truth of his conception of it, that in the long run he achieved so immense and lasting a success. For nothing about the *Book of Martyrs* is so impressive as the effectiveness with which it achieved its purpose. Its author told the Queen in his epistle dedicatory to her that he wanted to add to "the voice of Christ's gospel and faithful preaching of his word . . . the knowledge also of Ecclesiastical History which, in my mind, ought not to be separate from the same; that like as by the one the people may learn the rules and precepts of doctrine, so by the other they may have examples of God's mighty working in his church, to the confirmation of their faith and the edification of the Christian life".[28]

This was, in fact, precisely how Foxe's book came to be regarded in English popular opinion. He had set out to write an epic Protestant history which should be part of the indestructible core of the religious patrimony of the country. And he had succeeded. Partly because, for all his prolixity, he could write such vigorous, flexible and vivid English prose. Partly because, like many of his contemporaries, he had a sure instinct for the dramatic and could evoke with unforgettable effect the electrifying clash of idea and personality.

But, transcending all other explanations of his success, were the scope and unity of his theme. In it, past, present and future were all bound up together in a single coherent saga; majestic in meaning and over-whelming in impact. Here was profane history dovetailed neatly into sacred history; the episodes of English church history slotted firmly into the several acts of the universal drama of Christendom. Immersed from his youth in the content and spirit of biblical history and prophecy, Foxe found it the most natural thing in the world to carry its ethos over into British history. Britain, too, had its story of a compact between Jehovah and his chosen people, an elect nation enjoying a special relationship with the deity. As long as it performed his will, it had prospered. As soon as it had turned its back on him, disasters had ineluctably followed. Allowing itself to be subverted by Antichrist, it had fallen into a state of desolation. But, after centuries of darkness and Roman usurpation, God had sent true prophets again. From Wycliffe onwards, and especially in the age of the Reformation, he had wonder-fully raised up witnesses to the truth. By the blood and suffering of his martyrs he had sealed the triumph of his cause. This at least was how Foxe saw it and, such was the power of his pen and so strong the predisposition of his readers to believe him, that this, too, was the way that generations of them saw it.

On this showing, the wheel of ecclesiastical history had come full cycle from the persecution of the first Christian martyrs to those who had died in Mary's reign. The latter had died for no new-fangled sedition but for the same truth as the former.

> We have sufficiently proved, asserted Foxe, by the continual descent of the Church till this present time that the said church, after the doctrine which is now reformed, is no new-begun matter, but even the old continued Church by the providence and promise of Christ still standing.[29]

The reasons for the two outbursts of persecution were also, he believed, identical. Satan had been loose for three hundred years after Christ's birth seeking the destruction of his Church. One thousand years later he had been set at large again. Those cardinal Christian qualities which had defeated him in the early Christian era—constancy and valour for the true faith under the inspiration of heaven-sent prophets and princes —had been reborn in the sixteenth century.

Nor were these two great victories without a direct link of the utmost consequence as far as Britain was concerned. Foxe thought it no accident that Constantine, "the great and worthy emperor . . . was not only a Briton born . . . but also by the help of the British army (under the power of God) . . . obtained, with great victory, peace and tranquillity to the whole universal church of Christ".[30] What Constantine had achieved in the fourth century under divine providence, Elizabeth and her subjects, it might be hoped, had done in the sixteenth century. Modern historians, even those among them who are devout Christians, may find it hard not to smile more than a little wryly at the thought of the cool and worldly-wise Elizabeth being cast in such a role. But that does not lessen one whit the potency or the persuasiveness which that type-casting enshrined for her own subjects and many generations of their posterity. Foxe has almost unchallengeable claims to the title of prince of English historical myth-makers.

AFTERMATH AND CONCLUSIONS

ᴛ ᴡᴀꜱ ɴᴏᴛ only in England that such Protestant history was enthu-
iastically pursued. In Wales, Scotland and Ireland, too, it had its
exponents and its distinctive variations. The Welsh had a particularly
keen appetite for early British history and a strong sense of the unique
destiny of their own nation. Although their acceptance of reformed
doctrine had in general been tardy and reluctant, there nevertheless
existed a small group of Welshmen who were powerfully attracted by
it. Humanists and Oxford graduates, steeped also in the literary and
cultural heritage of Wales, they were prompted to re-examine the
history of their own people in the light of their reformed convictions.
The two key figures among them were Richard Davies, bishop of
St. David's (1561–81) and an exile for religion in Mary's reign, and
William Salesbury, the greatest Renaissance scholar produced in Wales.
This pair's interest and expertise were well known to Parker and Cecil,
with whom they exchanged a number of letters. The fullest exposition
of their version of early British church history was given in Bishop
Davies's *Address to the Welsh Nation* with which he prefaced their
translation of the New Testament, the first Welsh version, published
in 1567.[1]

Davies based his account to a large extent on Geoffrey of Monmouth's *Historia Regum*. But it was Geoffrey with a difference. Far from
emphasizing, as Geoffrey had done, the alleged temporal glory of the
ancient British, Davies concentrated exclusively on their highest claim
to distinction: their "uncorrupted religion". This they had first received
from Joseph of Arimathea. Later, Eleutherius had helped by sending
Fagan and Damian in response to King Lucius's appeal. After Lucius's
time, Davies contended, the Britons held fast to their faith as they had
first received it; this in the teeth of all the savage persecution which
Diocletian and other pagan tyrants unloosed upon it and in spite of all
the plausible wiles of Pelagians and other heretics. What ultimately
proved to be the Britons' undoing was the consequences of Augustine's
mission to the Anglo-Saxons. While the latter were still heathens the

Welsh were willing enough to traffic with them, or so Davies argued. But once the Saxons had been converted to Augustine's Roman version of Christianity so great was the Britons' abhorrence of its superstition that they would no longer have anything to do with them. Bent on keeping their own beliefs undesecrated, the Welsh remained rigidly aloof until they were eventually forced to accept papist abominations at the point of the sword.

The markedly nationalist hue with which Davies tinged his whole account of the early history may well have had a connexion with his desire to get rid of two of the most serious obstacles to the spread of Protestantism in Wales. These were the prejudice against it as a new-fangled heresy and as an English religion, uncongenial to Wales. The first of these objections was common enough in most European countries. Continental and English reformers had, from the beginnings of the Reformation, been obliged to rebut what Jewel called the "high brag" of their opponents that all "antiquity and a continual consent of all ages" was on their side, while Protestantism was "but new and yesterday's work".[2] Davies, however, felt confident of being able to prove that at the apogee of the ancient British kingdom the religion of its people had been firmly grounded on the reformers' rock of scriptural authority. This was the excellence that outweighed all their other claims to eminence. It was the priceless heritage they had been forced to relinquish, and evil days had come upon their posterity. Learning decayed, the scriptures in their own tongue were lost, and the proud descendants of Brutus were ground beneath the Saxon heel. But, at length, after centuries of darkness God in his infinite mercy had vouchsafed them a new opportunity of embracing, not a rootless error, but the ancient faith of their nation in its golden age.

Almost as devastating was the blow which Davies's account struck at those who held that the reformers' doctrine was something English and alien. He seemed to be turning the tables on them completely by showing that Romish religion, far from being in the national tradition of the Welsh, was something degrading imposed upon them by their enemies. He besought his nation to

> call to mind its ancient privilege and great honour, which sprang from its acceptance of the faith of Christ and the word of God, which it had received before all the islands of the world.

This was its true spiritual patrimony, something in which the English had never shared before the Reformation. In accepting the reformers' teaching, therefore, the Welsh would not be embracing an alien creed but reavailing themselves of their "once most glorious heritage".

In Scotland there was at first less concern for early church history than might have been expected in a country so deeply impressed by Protestant doctrine. The greatest of her sixteenth-century historians was that splendid scholar and Latin poet, George Buchanan, whose *Rerum Scoticarum Historia* was published in 1582, the last year of his life. In this weighty and ambitious work, informed throughout with a critical scholarly sense that put to shame many of his English contemporaries, Buchanan was not specially concerned with church history. His object was to chronicle an orthodox secular history of Scotland. However, from time to time he revealed his reforming sympathies in the way he referred to individual events or personalities. Of Augustine of Canterbury, for example, he had this to say:

> qui sua ambitione, dum novam religionem docet, veterem vehementer turbavit: nam non tam Christianam disciplinam quam caerimonias Romanas docebat. Superiores enim Britanni, Christianissmum ex Joannis Evangelistae discipulis edocti, a monachis, quos aetas illa adhuc eruditos et pios habebat instituebantur . . . disciplinam, jam in superstitionem prolabentem, ita caerimonis novis, fictisque miraculis, oppressit, ut sincerae pietatis vix relinqueret vestigium.[3]

Buchanan further betrays his religious sympathies when he treated of those Scottish kings who appeared to have defied papal authority, for example, King William's opposition to Pope Alexander III or the popular support accorded to Robert Bruce in defiance of the pope's hostility to him. His silence on other occasions could be more eloquent than his testimony. For instance, he has no mention of Pope Celestine III's action of 1192 which made Scotland a "special daughter of Rome", nor of the papal bull *Quidam Vestrum* of 1225 which reinforced the special relationship of Scotland to the papacy. Yet, on the whole, that characteristic and enormously persuasive idea of an autonomous national church in Scotland finds relatively very little support in Buchanan or the authors of the sixteenth century. It was later, in the next two centuries, that this notion took root and blossomed profusely in Scotland. Thereafter, the concept of a "Scottish church, national and anti-papal, a continuous entity from the sixth to the nineteenth century, was an expression not so much of the popular mind as of the popular will".[4]

It was in the seventeenth century, too, that Archbishop Ussher, in addition to upholding the Protestant view of the history of the early

E

Church in Britain, went to great lengths to clear the early Irish Church from any possible taint of papistry. He attributed to Polydore Vergil the origin of the supposition that the pope enjoyed temporal power over Ireland by virtue of a special grant made to him at the time of its first conversion. Ussher dismissed this with the usual reformer's innuendo that Polydore

> being sent over by the pope into England for the collecting of his Peter-pence, undertook the writing of the history of that nation; wherein he forgat not by the way to do the best service he could to his lord that had employed him thither.

Ussher would go no further than to admit that St. Patrick had a "special regard unto the Church of Rome, from whence he was sent for the conversion of this island", a regard which Ussher concedes he himself would have had for Rome in those, its undefiled, days. Any such regard could not, however, be binding for the future:

> But that St Patrick was of opinion that the Church of Rome was sure ever afterward to continue in that good estate, and that there was a perpetual privilege annexed unto that see, that it should never err in judgment, or that the pope's sentences were always to be held as infallible oracles; that will I never believe.[5]

Nor could he ever believe other than that the "religion professed by the ancient bishops, priests, monks, and other Christians in this land" was for substance the very same with that which was in his own day "by public authority maintained therein, against the foreign doctrine brought in thither in latter times by the bishop of Rome's followers".[6]

In all four countries of the British Isles, therefore, the crux of the argument for the existence of an early national church, scriptural and unstained in creed and practice, was necessarily the same. It rested on three postulates. First, Britain had been chosen specially early by divine providence for initial conversion during apostolic times by Joseph of Arimathea, who had established Christ's teaching direct from its well-spring without imperfection or adulteration. Second, that faith had been resolutely maintained unsubverted in face of persecution by the Roman Emperors and the errors of Pelagians and other heretics. Contact with the bishop of Rome there may indeed have been at some points during these centuries, but Rome itself was at this stage unblemished by ambition or superstition. Third, throughout the period of pagan Saxon invasions the Christians of the north and west had held fast to their beliefs and maintained close contact with one another.

When finally they had been brought face to face with the Roman mission of Augustine of Canterbury they had put up a godly front of opposition both to his arrogant claim of overlordship and to the superstitious innovations he had tried to introduce. Ultimately obliged by force of arms to accept Roman authority as a punishment for their own sins they had, thereafter, been able to make only sporadic and mainly unsuccessful protests against the encroachments of Antichrist until the "second flowering of the gospel" in Reformation times. Such theories were not by any means wholly without foundation. They had a sufficient basis in fact to make them plausible as well as attractive and even necessary from the reformers' point of view.

*   *   *

During the seventeenth, eighteenth, and even nineteenth centuries British historians continued to retain the essentials of the theory of an early Protestant Church in Britain, although better-informed and more critical scholarship pruned it of its more palpably mythical accretions. Thus, for example, the legends about Joseph of Arimathea were disposed of in the honest atmosphere of the best seventeenth-century scholarship.[7] It was left to Edward Stillingfleet, bishop of Worcester, finally to dispose of the whole story in 1685 in his *Origines Britannicae*. Yet although he was willing to demolish one myth, Stillingfleet himself was no less anxious than his predecessors had been to provide the Church in Britain with an apostolic founder. He put forward St. Paul as the founder of the British Church. The proofs he offered in support, miserably thin by modern standards, seemed strong enough at the time to be accepted by Protestant historians down to the middle of the nineteenth century.

Similarly, though a second-century British king like Lucius, ruling in the midst of a Roman province, appeared so improbable a figure to thoughtful antiquarians, it was not until well into the nineteenth century that he was finally banished from the historical scene. Long before that, his presence had provoked uneasy headshakings. The difficulty of finding a consistent chronology which would have enabled him to be fitted into the pontificate of Eleutherius was noted by a number of authors from Ussher onwards. An equally awkward problem was raised by the need to explain away the remarkable phenomenon of his anomalous position with regard to the imperial authorities. Not even by 1839 had Lucius been entirely exorcized. In that year M. A. Tierney, in his edition of *Dodd's Church History*, wrote, "Of the precise motives

67

which influenced the conduct of Lucius on this occasion, we can know nothing. The facts, however, remain undisputed."[8]

It was very slowly, too, that the prejudice against Augustine disappeared. Protestants deplored his pride and were sceptical of his miracles. It was a long time before they completely exonerated him from complicity in Ethelred's massacre of the Welsh monks, though Foxe had long since given him the benefit of what slight doubt there was.[9]

The deadly threat to church and state which earnest Anglicans saw in the demands for Catholic emancipation at the beginning of the nineteenth century gave a new significance in the eyes of many to the notion of an early Protestant church. It now became for them the most telling argument on behalf of maintaining the establishment and one which, if properly used, could be fatal to the sophistry of those papists who maintained that theirs was after all the true ancient faith of Britain. Nowhere was the idea of an early Protestant church more fervently proclaimed than in Bishop Burgess's *Tracts on the Origin and Independence of the Ancient British Church* . . . (1815). Bishop of St. David's from 1803 to 1825, Burgess had not the slightest doubt that the ancient church of Britain had been a "Protestant Church nine centuries before the days of Luther". "The popery of Britain", he asserted confidently, constituted "the *middle ages* of the British church. Down to the beginning of the seventh century there was no trace of popery. . . . From the reign of Henry I to the middle of that of Henry VIII (1115–1530) was the period of her subjection to the Pope. This, he believed, ought to convince any "unprejudiced mind that Popery obtained no establishment in this country but by usurpation".[10] Much the same point of view was put by Henry Soames a generation later in his influential book, *The Anglo-Saxon Church* (1835).

It was in the context of increasingly spirited exchanges of the same kind that Foxe's *Book of Martyrs* came under heavy critical fire. Much of his exegesis of early British church history had, of course, long become as porous as that of his contemporaries and had ceased to hold water. But his account of the sixteenth-century Reformation struggles and his contribution to the image of "God's Englishmen" had continued to exert powerful and pervasive influence. Taken alongside Sir Edward Coke's equally seminal myth of the political liberties of early Englishmen, which was held to be the secular counterpart of their religious freedom during the same period, it laid the foundations of what has since become known as the "Whig interpretation" of English history. Moreover, its radical overtones had given added conviction and backbone to English radicals. "Lilburne, Walwyn and Overton looked back to medieval heretics and Marian martyrs as their direct ancestors", and the same inspiration gave Cromwell his assurance of victory at Naseby.[11] But by the age of the Tractarian controversies the *Book of Martyrs* had become the bone of such contention that the editor of a standard nineteenth-century edition of it could describe it in these terms: "The approbation or the disapprobation of the great principles of the *Acts and Monuments* of John Foxe is now too often made the criterion of attachment, or non-attachment, to the Church of England itself."[12] So severely indeed was Foxe's authority mauled that his reputation in scholarly circles remained mutilated almost beyond redemption for a very long time afterwards, as we have already seen.

By our own day the passage of time and the emergence of diametrically different conceptions of history have softened the sharp edges of controversy between sixteenth-century Reformers and their opponents and have thrown into relief their underlying similarity. From our point of view the contribution of the Protestants to historical scholarship does not appear impressively original. As far as historical method went they did help to give the study of the subject valuable impetus. The main impulse in the search for old books and manuscripts and in their preservation came from them. They also injected a powerful stimulus into the process of the scholarly ransacking of ancient authorities for new evidence concerning church history. But this avidity for historical material was created at least as much by the Renaissance as by the Reformation; and when it came to handling the evidence there were occasions when the Protestant historians showed themselves to be too medievally minded to accept the findings of more discriminating Renaissance scholarship, the outstanding example being their ill-founded defence of Geoffrey of Monmouth's work against the "Roman" iconoclasm of Polydore Vergil.

Nor could the Reformers abandon the classical Christian conception of human history as part of a mighty cosmic drama, in which the creation of the world and the incarnation of Christ were the most significant episodes, and final redemption the end to which all history was moving. They laid particular emphasis on the fact that the only authentic revelation of that eternal plan, of which human history was the unfolding, was to be found in the Bible. So it was not surprising that the relations between Jehovah and his people disclosed in sacred history should have coloured all their thinking about secular history and that their supreme concern was to find in it evidence of obedience to God being followed by prosperity, and deviation from His paths no less surely bringing disaster in its train. Within the framework of the Christian viewpoint, therefore, there was room for considerable difference of opinion in emphasis and in detail if not in fundamentals. The Protestants' account of the rise of the papacy, for example, was very revealing. They had a shrewd appreciation of the work of the great popes, even if they did detest their achievements. Unhampered by the need to justify every enlargement of papal authority as fulfilment of a divine purpose they had a clearer sight of the human frailty that often underlay it, though of course they went too far in the other direction by attributing the whole diabolical phenomenon to the machinations of the Prince of Darkness.

They left their mark on British history, too, though many of their most cherished opinions have been scattered like chaff before the wind of modern historiography. The Joseph of Arimathea legend and the Eleutherius story have long since been decently buried, and few would any longer be found to see in Augustine's quarrel with the Welsh bishops evidence of a proto-Protestant opposition to papal encroachment. Yet, however unhistorically they may have viewed the Celtic Church in some respects, their insistence that its representatives were rightfully proud of their own religious patrimony was of permanent value, for indeed the Celts were not mere backwoodsmen rejecting Rome and clinging to their own tradition from nothing but ignorance and stubborn prejudice. Or again, for instance, the Protestants' emphasis on the links that bound them to the Lollards was not wholly misconceived. It may not be possible any longer to accept John Wycliffe as the "Morning Star of the Reformation", but the most recent scholarship confirms the importance of Lollard survivals in early Tudor England and the connexion between them and the growth of Reformation opinion.

What has not lasted has been the sixteenth-century sense of the immanence of God in the historical process. There is no longer the same intense certainty of opinion on the nature of His intervention in all human events. There is now—among historians at least—no painful detailed scrutiny of past and present for the minute and unmistakable working out of the divine will in accordance with a traceable and immutable grand design already charted in the Scriptures. Some flavour of the continuing attraction of the appeal of this kind of hypothesizing

70

can still be savoured by anyone who has the interest—and the temerity —to read the literature of some of the more literalist Christian sects or, even better, to engage in a dialogue with their adherents. Given the general disinclination of historians, however, to indulge in any attempts to delineate divine intervention in this fashion, the sixteenth century's confidence that it could re-create a quasi-scriptural frame of reference of obedience to the Almighty's fiat and rebellion against it, has long since withered. Modern historians, including those among them who are Christians and primarily interested in the history of the Church, would hesitate long before claiming to be able neatly to pigeon-hole either the relationship of men's actions to God's will or the consequences which the nature of such a relationship might have provoked. In taking up such a standpoint they would not wish to ignore the deep and genuine convictions which made the reformers' attitude to history particularly relevant to the age in which they lived. John Foxe was, as Dr. T. H. L. Parker has aptly pointed out, writing against the "whole nest of Epicures" with the intention of stressing particularly the "God's mighty working in the life of man". It was of the utmost consequence to him to maintain his basic premise that the course of all human history was God-directed. In the sixteenth-century context, as Dr. Parker has rightly argued, this was far from childish and it had "a reputable tradition and a sensible motive".[13] It was, indeed, an integral part of the defence of Christian belief. Many modern Christian historians would certainly not deny that such divine direction exists and has always existed. They would accept that God's hand can be traced in history. But honesty would nevertheless compel them to admit that any enquiry directed into such problems on the basis of a modern historian's techniques and presuppositions can produce answers of only very limited validity.

There have been powerful reasons why the earlier more confident assessments of the role of God in history with which we have been concerned in previous chapters did not retain their full vigour far beyond the intensely theologically minded age of the Reformation itself. The cooler, more sceptical temper of the later seventeenth century and the eighteenth left its mark on church history, too, and evidence was not wanting of a more rationalist interpretation of church history in terms primarily of human causes. That trend has, in the last century and this one, been strengthened for a variety of reasons. These cannot be adequately discussed at the fag-end of a short book of this kind; but it may help briefly to note some of them.

The immense elongation of the time-scale of planetary existence by geology, biology and related sciences has not only appeared drastically to reduce the status of man in the order of created things; it has also shattered that cosy continuum of five or six thousand years of human history based on a literal interpretation of the Bible which gave to a century of history, or even the life-span of an average individual, a possible significance in the chronological scheme of things far greater than it would now be likely to assume.

A comparable broadening of horizons as the result of the work of archaeologists, anthropologists and students of comparative religion has also made it impossible to assign to the three-stranded civilization of European Christendom deriving from Judaea, Greece and Rome the unique primacy it once enjoyed as the focus of ecclesiastical and cultural historians' attention.

But what, most of all, would seem to have eroded the earlier confidence has been the changed attitude towards the Scriptures as a consequence, not only of the advance made in the sciences already mentioned, but also as a result of the higher criticism and a more searching analysis of the Bible itself. Such studies do not oblige Christians to abandon their belief in the ultimate value of the Bible as the revelation of the nature of God and his purposes. But they have made it impossible for many to regard the Bible as a straightforward literal record of events. Holy Writ can no longer be regarded as an indispensable cipher enabling mortals to decode the supernatural message of history, sacred and profane. What it has to communicate may be regarded as a more profound symbolic truth, but it is also inevitably a much more blurred and uncertain one as expressed by the working out of human destinies. What were once thought of as unmistakable and incontrovertible truths concerning what constituted God's work and the Devil's, Christ's régime and Antichrist's, chosen races and Ishmaelites throughout all human history must now be regarded as infinitely less certain quantities, even for Christian historians. For non-Christian historians such categories could at best be regarded as an outmoded irrelevance, at worst dangerous nonsense.

All this has made history, even church history, de-theologized in most of its assumptions and all its methods. Church historians may still start from the premise that the function of their study is to confirm their theological preconceptions. There is nothing disgraceful in that; many other historians have equally strong preconceptions of a different sort. But contemporary church historians cannot ignore the existence of well-established disciplines for the study of history. They are anxious that their work should measure up to the most rigorous critique of ordinary secular historical study. They want their findings to be acceptable, as far as their technical soundness goes, to believers and non-believers alike. This normally means that their explanation of the course of events is grounded in human motives and actions without recourse to supernatural causation or predestined fulfilment. The failures of the Church are accounted for in terms of the weakness or wickedness of its members and any awareness of an extra-terrestrial conspiracy on the part of the Evil One can be no more than implicit. Nor is a revival in the fortunes of the Church, or any section of it, explained as being brought about by a direct intervention from on high by a deity who willed either that he would no longer inflict punishment on men for their earlier sins or that he would no longer suffer their continued rebellion. On the contrary, such a revival is now represented as the outcome of a long-maturing process of changing human need and circumstance. Indeed, there have been times when the Reformation has been explained as having come about on account of all kinds of human concern except men's need to satisfy their religious longings.

So we have to conclude, then, that as far as their "technical" history is concerned, church historians—and indeed all others—do not find it obligatory to include among their working hypotheses the operation of divine providence. For this purpose, they can, like practising scientists, dispense with it. But this does not dispose of the profoundest questions which the men of the sixteenth century were trying to answer. The present-day historian, if he is a believer, still has to put to himself such issues as the relationship of human history to divine predetermination or the manner and meaning of the ways in which earthly happenings are shaped by God. Just as a scientist-believer has to ask himself how the universe and its laws embody the presence and purpose of God. Both kinds of believers—historians and scientists—may find that the intellectual disciplines to which they are committed yield them no more than a penultimate explanation of why things happen and God's creatures behave as they have done and still do. Any ultimate explanation they give will come from sources outside their technical studies. They will come from the realm of faith and personal experience.

In that respect their inspiration will in essentials be the same as that of the Reformation historians. They, too, brought their deepest convictions *to* their study of the past and did not derive them *from* it. The conviction of contemporary historians, like those of the reformers, may be confirmed by their knowledge of history. But any confirmation thus forthcoming will, in our own day, be much more tentative and confused than the sharply drawn blue-print which Reformation historiography claimed to produce. The men of the sixteenth century were not wrong in asserting, as they did, that God rules history and that human destinies lie in His keeping. Nor were they mistaken in trying to discover and demonstrate His intentions. No sincere Christian could abandon such concepts without largely destroying his religious beliefs. But where the earlier historians were misguided was in the convictions—not unintelligible or unreasonable within the context of their own times—that they could nearly always determine why and when the divine intervention had occurred in the past and how, based on a too-literal reading of the Book of Revelation, it would take place in the future.

In our own day and age we must be content with a much lesser degree of certainty. That seems inevitable and is not necessarily deplorable. For if we think that God's intentions for men are such that they can be comprehended in sum and detail by mortal and finite beings we fall into the danger of conceiving of a deity unworthily limited in scope and nature by the shortcomings of human understanding.

BIBLIOGRAPHY

In THE bibliography below details are given of the most important works by Tyndale, Bale and Foxe which are discussed in the text of this volume. In the notes which follow the bibliography I have given references to convenient and accessible modern editions of these sixteenth-century books wherever they exist. The notes also provide bibliographical information for all references to other primary and secondary sources cited.

WILLIAM TYNDALE

The obediēce of a Christen man and how Christē rulers ought to governe, where in also (yf thou marke diligently) thou shalt fynde eyes to perceave the crafty conveyaūce of all iugglers.

> Hans luft: at Marlborow in the lāde of Hesse, 1528 (?Antwerp)

The practyse of Prelates. Whether the Kynges grace maye be separated from hys quene, because she was his brothers wyfe.

> Marborch, 1530 (?Antwerp)

A treatyse of the iustificacyon by faith only, otherwise called the parable of the wyked Mammon.

> Printed . . . for James Nycolson: Southwarke, 1536

JOHN BALE

A brefe Chronycle concernynge the Examinacyon and death of the blessed martyr of Christ syr John Oldecastell the lorde Cobham, etc.

> (?Antwerp), 1544

The first examinacyon of Anne Askewe latelye martyred in Smythfelde by the Romysh Popes upholders, with the elucydacyon of Johan Bale.

> 1546

The Actes of Englysh Votaryes comprehendynge their vnchast practyses and examples by all ages, from the worldes begynnynge to thys present yeare, collected out of theire owne legendes and chronycles (the first parte).

> Wesel, 1546 (?John Day, London, 1546)

The first two partes of the Actes or vnchast examples of the Englysh votaryes, gathered out of their owne legenades and Chronycles by Johan

Bale, and dedycated to our [r]edoubted soueraigne kynge Edward the syxte.

Thomas Raynalde, London, 1548

Illustrium Maioris Britanniae scriptorum, hoc est, Angliae, Cambriae, ac Scotiae summariū, in quasdam centurias diuisum, cum diuersitate doctrinarū atq.; annorū recta supputatione per omnes aetates a Iapheto sanctissimi Noah filio, ad annum domini M.D.XLVIII.

Ioannem Ouerton: Guppeswici, 1548 (D. van Streten: Wesel, in reality)

The image of bothe churches after the moste wonderfull and heauenly Reuelacion of Sainct John the Euangelist, contayning a very frutefull exposicion or paraphrase upon the same, Wherein it is conferred with the other scripturs, and most auctorised historyes. Compyled by John Bale an exile also in this life for the faythfull testimonie of Jesu.

(?1548)

Acta Romanorum Pontificum, à dispersione discipulorum Christi, usque ad tempora Pauli quarti, qui nunc in Ecclesia tyrannizat: Ex Ioannis Balei Sudouolgij Angli maiore Catalogo Anglicorum Scriptorum desumpta, & in tres Classes, Libros Verò semptem (sic) diuisa ... Adiectus est.

Ex officina Oporini: Basileae, 1558

The Pageant of Popes, contayninge the lyues of all the Bishops of Rome, from the beginninge of them to the yeare of Grace 1555 ... Written in Latin by Maister Bale, and now Englished with sondrye additions by I.S. (Iohn Studley).

Thomas Marshe: London, 1574

A Newe Comedy or Enterlude concernying thre lawes, of Nature, Moises, and Christe, etc.

Thomas Colwell, London, 1562

JOHN FOXE

Commentarii rerum in ecclesia gestarum, maximarumque, per totam Europam persecutionum, à Vuiclevi temporibus ad hanc usque aetatē descriptio. Liber primus ... Hiis in calce accesserunt Aphorismi J. Vuiclevi, cum collectaneis quibusdam, R. Pecoki Episcopi Cicestrensis, etc.

V. Rihelius: Argentorati, 1554

Actes and monuments of these latter and perillous dayes, touching matters of the Church, wherein ar comprehended and described the great peresecutions & horrible troubles, that have bene wrought and practised by the Romishe prelates, speciallye in this Realme of England and Scotlande, from the yeare of our Lorde, a thousande, unto the tyme nowe present. Gathered and collected according to the true copies & wrytinges certificatorie.

John Day: London, 1563

The first (-second) volume of the Ecclesiasticall History, contayning the

76

Actes and Monumentes of thynges passed in every kynges tyme in this realme, especially in the Church of England . . . Newly . . . inlarged by the author.

2 volumes, London, 1570

The first (-second) volume of the Ecclesiasticall history, contayning the actes & monumentes of thinges passed in every kinges time in this realme, especially in the Church of England . . . With a full discourse of such persecutions, horrible troubles, the suffring of martirs . . . and other thinges incident, touching as well the sayde Church of England, as also, Scotland, and all other forrein nations, from the primitive time, till the reigne of King Henry the Eyght.

The Second volume . . . contayning the . . . Acts & Monumentes of Martyrs . . . from the time of K. Henry the VIII to Queene Elizabeth.) Newly recognised and inlarged by the author.

John Daye: London, 1576

NOTES

I

THE CONTINENTAL BACKGROUND

1. J. M. Robertson (ed.), *The Philosophical Works of Francis Bacon* (London, 1927), p. 2.

2. Quoted in R. H. Bainton, *Here I Stand: A Life of Martin Luther* (New York, 1955), p. 88.

3. Quoted in Karl Brandi, *The Emperor Charles V* (London, 1965), p. 131.

4. Quoted in Bainton, *op. cit.*, p. 150.

5. H. Bullinger, *Decades* (4 vols., Parker Society, 1852), IV, pp. 532–33.

6. John Calvin, *Institutes of the Christian Religion*, transl. H. Beveridge (2 vols., London, 1953), II, pp. 427–28.

7. James Westfall Thompson, *A History of Historical Writing* (2 vols., New York, 1942), I, p. 531.

8. Bullinger, *Decades*, IV, p. 89.

9. Calvin, *Institutes*, II, pp. 377–78.

10. J. M. Headley, *Luther's View of Church History* (Yale University Press, 1963), p. 221.

11. F. H. Littel, *The Anabaptist View of the Church* (American Society of Church History, 1952), p. 63.

II

THE ENGLISH PIONEER: WILLIAM TYNDALE

1. R. Demaus, *William Tyndale* (London, 1871), p. 41.

2. Quoted in J. F. Mozley, *William Tyndale* (S.P.C.K., 1937), p. 8.

3. William Tyndale, *Works* (3 vols., Parker Society, 1848–50), I, p. 399; cf. also I, pp. 449–50.

4. *Ibid.*, I, pp. 142–43.

5. *Ibid.*, I, p. 450; for the whole prologue to the Book of Jonah, I, pp. 449–66.

6. *Ibid.*, I, pp. 458–59.

7. W. A. Clebsch, *England's Earliest Protestants, 1520–1535* (Yale Univ. Press, New Haven, 1964), pp. 199, 203.

8. Tyndale, *Works*, I, pp. 42–43.

9. *Ibid.*, I, p. 42.

10. *The Practice of Prelates* is printed in full in Tyndale's *Works*, II, pp. 240–344.

11. *Ibid.*, II, p. 296.

12. *Ibid.*, II, p. 257.

13. *Ibid.*

14. *Works*, I, p. 458.

15. *Ibid.*, I, p. 459.

16. *Ibid.*, I, p. 140.

17. John Bale, *Select Works* (Parker Society, 1849), p. 6.

III

THE LINK: JOHN BALE

1. H. Ellis, *Original Letters illustrative of English History* (11 vols., London, 1824–46), III, p. 154.

2. J. W. Harris, *John Bale: a Study in the Minor Literature of the Reformation* (University of Illinois, Urbana, 1940), p. 37.

3. *The Dramatic Works of John Bale*, ed. J. S. Farmer (Early English Dramatists Series, 1907), pp. 64–65.

4. *Ibid.*, pp. 223–24.

5. *Ibid.*, p. 199.

6. *Ibid.*, p. 272.

7. Quoted in Harris, *Bale*, p. 126.

8. Bale, *Select Works*, p. 8.

9. *English Votaries*, I, pp. 23*v.*–26.

10. *Ibid.*, p. 78.

11. *Ibid.*, II, p. 55.

12. Cf. also "Examination of Anne Askew", *Select Works*, pp. 190–93.

13. *English Votaries*, II, p. 116.

14. *The Pageant of Popes*, transl. by John Studley and published in 1574, p. 15.

15. *Ibid.*, p. 24*v.*

16. *Ibid.*, p. 72.

17. *Ibid.*, p. 113*v.*

18. William Haller, *Foxe's Book of Martyrs and the Elect Nation* (London, 1963), p. 64.

19. Bale, *Select Works*, p. 18. *The Image of Both Churches* is published in full in *Select Works*, pp. 249–640.

20. *Ibid.*, p. 252.

21. *Ibid.*

22. *Ibid.*, pp. 188–89.
23. *Ibid.*, p. 15.
24. *Ibid.*, p. 140.
25. *Ibid.*, p. 6.
26. *Ibid.*, p. 406.

IV

THE CONSUMMATION: JOHN FOXE

1. E. Grindal, *Remains* (Parker Society, 1843), p. 240.
2. See M. Parker, *Correspondence* (Parker Society, 1853), *passim*, and especially pp. 425–26.
3. *Ibid.*, p. 327.
4. W. W. Greg, "Books and bookmen in the correspondence of Archbishop Parker", *The Library*, XVI (1935), pp. 247ff.
5. See especially John Jewel, *Works* (Parker Society, 1845–50), I, pp. 345–46; II, pp. 686–87; and IV, p. 778.
6. *The Second Replie . . . agaynst Master Doctor Whitgift's Second Answer* (London, 1575), p. 475; for Whitgift's own position see his *Works* (Parker Society, 1851–53), pp. 128–30.
7. John Foxe, *Actes and Monuments* . . . Ed. G. Townsend and S. R. Cattley (8 vols., London, 1841), I, p. 504.
8. Eusebius, *The History of the Church*, transl. G. A. Williamson (Pelican Books, 1965), p. 192.
9. *Ibid.*
10. Foxe, I, pp. 522–23.
11. Foxe, I, p. 514.
12. Foxe, III, p. 323.
13. Foxe, III, p. 377.
14. Foxe, I, pp. 4–5.
15. Foxe, II, pp. 724–27.
16. Foxe, II, p. 796.
17. Foxe, I, p. 5.
18. Foxe, II, p. 356.
19. Foxe, I, p. 5.
20. Foxe, I, pp. 310–11.
21. Foxe, II, p. 169.
22. Foxe, II, p. 791.
23. Eusebius, *History*, p. 327.
24. Foxe, I, p. 521.
25. William Haller, *Foxe's Book of Martyrs and the Elect Nation* (London, 1963), p. 215.

26. Foxe, III, p. 98.

27. Foxe, VIII, pp. 625-28.

28. Foxe, I, p. 504.

29. Foxe, I, pp. 519-20.

30. Foxe, I, p. 312.

V

AFTERMATH AND CONCLUSIONS

1. An English translation of this address may be found in A. O. Evans, *A Memorandum on the Legality of the Welsh Bible* (Cardiff, 1925), pp. 83-124.

2. Jewel, *Works*, III, p. 84.

3. George Buchanan, *Opera Omnia* (2 vols., Edinburgh, 1715), I, pp. 85-86.

4. M. V. Hay, *A Chain of Error in Scottish History* (London, 1927), p. 67.

5. James Ussher, *A Discourse of the Religion Anciently Professed by the Irish and the British* (London, 1631), pp. 89, 65-66.

6. *Ibid.*, introduction, no pagination.

7. For further details see the present writer's "Some Protestant views of early British church history", *History*, XXXVIII (1953), pp. 218-33.

8. Quoted by T. D. Kendrick, *British Antiquity* (London, 1950), p. 113.

9. See, for example, Thomas Fuller, *The Church History of Britain* (London, 1655), pp. 53-54, 68.

10. Thomas Burgess, *op. cit.*, p. 279 and *passim*.

11. Christopher Hill, *Intellectual Origins of the English Revolution* (Oxford, 1965), pp. 179-80.

12. George Townsend, *Acts and Monuments*, I, p. 232.

13. In a letter to the author dated July 10, 1967. Cf. also Dr. Parker's admirably concise and thoughtful treatment of these problems in their relation to John Foxe's work in his *English Reformers* (Volume XXVI, The Library of Christian Classics, S.C.M., 1966), pp. 61-68.

INDEX

Acta Romanorum Pontificum, 40–2
Acts of English Votaries, 38–40, 42, 50
Address to the Welsh Nation, 63–4
Albigensians, 56
Alexander III, pope, 65
America, North, 21
Anabaptists, 15, 19
Anglicans, 15, 68
Anglo-Saxon Church, The, 68
Annales Ecclesisastici, 13
Anselm, 27, 40, 57–8
Antichrist, 12, 14, 17, 18, 20, 26, 27,
    28, 29, 38, 39, 40, 41, 42, 43, 44,
    51, 54–5, 61, 67, 72
Antwerp, 23
Apostles, the, 8, 9, 12, 16, 18, 19, 20,
    39, 41, 47, 50
Askew, Anne, 44
Augustine, St., of Canterbury, 39, 47,
    60, 63–4, 65, 67, 68, 70
Augustine, St., of Hippo, 13, 16, 43

Bacon, Francis, 7
Bale, John, 27, 31, 32, 33–45, 46, 49,
    50, 51, 56, 60
Baptism, adult, 18
Barnes, Robert, 8, 33, 41
Baronius, Cardinal, 13
Basle, 34, 49
Becket, Thomas, 27, 53
Bible, 13, 16, 25, 38, 48, 69, 72
    English, 23
    Geneva, 46
Boniface III, pope, 17, 26, 41, 54
Boston, Lincs., 49
Britain, 39, 40, 47, 56, 57, 61, 62, 66,
    67, 68

British Isles, 66
Britons, early, 24, 25, 28, 39, 49, 57,
    63–4
Bruce, Robert, 65
Buchanan, George, 65
Bullinger, Heinrich, 10, 11, 17
Burgess, Thomas, 68

Calvin, John, 11, 12, 16, 17
Calvinists, 15, 21
Cambridge, university of, 22, 33
    Jesus College, 33
Canterbury, 34
    archbishops of, 27, 34, 46
Capgrave, John, 39
Carmelite friars, 33
Cartwright, Thomas, 47–8
Catalogus, Bale's, 37, 38, 50
Catholics, 13
Cecil, William, 63
Celestine III, pope, 65
Celtic Church, 70
Centuries of Magdeburg, 12, 51
Charles V, emperor, 8
Christ, Jesus, 12, 13, 16, 24, 25, 26, 30,
    39, 40, 41, 42, 43, 44, 50, 54, 55,
    57, 58, 60, 62, 64, 66, 69
Christendom, 8, 9, 16, 54, 55, 61, 72
Christianity, 9, 13, 26, 39, 47, 54, 64
Christians, 9, 13, 62, 66, 71–2
Chronicles, chroniclers, 7, 28, 38, 43,
    51, 53, 56, 57
    English, 23, 27, 28, 36, 37, 38, 40,
    53
Chronicle of Lord Cobham, The, 38
Clergy, 28
Coke, Edward, 68

Constantine, emperor, 19, 20, 54, 62
  Donation, of 26
Constantinople, 17
Cope, Alan (i.e. Harpsfield, Nicholas), 53
Cranmer, Thomas, 22, 33
Cromwell, Thomas, 33

Damian, 57, 63
Davies, Richard, 63–4
De Antiquitate, 47
Decades, Bullinger's, 10, 11
Devil, the, 12, 14, 26, 41, 44, 72
Dodd's Church History, 67
Dunstan, 40
Dunwich, 33

Eck, John, 7, 8
Edward VI, king, 34, 46
Eleutherius, pope, 48, 57, 63, 67, 70
Elizabeth I, 34, 48, 50, 52, 57, 60, 62
Elizabethan church, 14
  England, 45, 46, 48, 52
England, 10, 23, 25, 28, 29, 30, 34, 36, 37, 38, 39, 43, 46, 49, 50, 54, 55, 56, 57–8, 59, 63, 66
  church of, 27, 42, 54, 69
Europe, 21, 22, 44, 54, 55
Eusebius, 13, 19, 43, 50–1, 56, 58

Fagan, 57, 63
Fathers, early, 8, 10, 12, 16
Foxe, John, 27, 34, 45, 46–62, 68–9, 71
France, 29
Franck, Sebastian, 20
Fraticelli, 20

Geneva, 46
Geoffrey of Monmouth, 48, 53, 63, 69
Germany, 11, 23, 29, 34, 51
Gildas, 24, 25, 28
God, 7, 9, 12, 13, 14, 15, 16, 18, 24, 25, 26, 28, 29, 38, 41, 43, 49, 55, 61,
    62, 64, 70, 71–4
  city of, 21, 43
Gregory I ('the Great'), pope, 17, 39, 42, 47
  VII, pope, 17, 42, 54
Grindal, Edmund, 46, 49

Hall, Edward, chronicler, 45, 53
Haller, Prof. William, 42–3, 49, 59
Henry I, king, 68
  IV, king, 40
  VIII, king 30, 36, 40, 43, 46, 49, 52, 59, 68
Heresy, heretics, 17–18, 20, 23, 56, 57, 63, 64, 66, 69
  Pelagian, 63, 66
Hildebrande, 17, 54
Holinshed, Raphael, chronicler, 45
Holy Ghost, Holy Spirit, 16, 19, 39
Huss, John, 18, 20, 53, 54, 56

Illyricus, Matthias Flacius, 12, 38, 42, 51
Image of Both Churches, The, 42–3
Innocent III, pope, 42, 54
  IV, pope, 41
Institutes of the Christian Religion, The, 11
Ireland, 34, 63, 66
Islam, 55

Jehovah, 61, 69
Jerusalem, the New, 43
Jewel, John, 47, 64
Jewel's *Defence*, 47
John, king, 28, 36
John VIII, pope, 41
Jonah, Book of, 25, 29
Joseph of Arimathea, 39, 44, 63, 66, 67, 70
Julius II, pope, 41

King John, 31, 36, 40

Latimer, Hugh, 22, 33
Legenda Aurea, 25
Leipzig, 7
Leland, John, 30–1, 33, 37, 38
Lollards, Lollardy, 29, 30, 44, 51, 56, 70
London, 23
Lucius, king of Britain, 48, 57, 63, 67–8
Luther, Martin, 7, 8, 9, 10, 14, 16, 20, 22, 23, 25, 42, 49, 56, 68
Lutherans, 15

Mark, St., 19
Martyrology, martyrs, 30, 34, 44, 46, 50–1, 53–6, 58–9, 60–1, 69
Martyrs, Book of, Foxe's, 45, 48–61, 68–9
Mary I, queen, 34, 43, 46, 58, 59, 60, 61, 63
Matthew, St., 19
Maurice, emperor, 17
Melanchthon, Philip, 10
Middle Ages, the, 21, 57
More, Sir Thomas, 23

New Testament, 11, 16, 18, 19, 20, 26, 50
  English, 23
  Welsh, 63
Norwich, 33

Obedience of a Christian Man, The, 24, 26, 28, 31
Oldcastle, Sir John, 30, 31, 44, 45
Old Testament, 21, 25, 26, 50, 59
On the Babylonish Captivity of the Church, 14
Origines Britannicae, 67
Ossory, 34
Ottoman Turks, 55, 56
Oxford, university of, 22, 49, 63
  Brasenose College, 49
  Magdalen College, 49

Pageant of the Popes, The, 41–2
Papacy, popes, 8, 9, 11, 12, 17, 20, 25, 27, 29, 31, 36, 37, 38, 39, 40–2, 51, 55, 58, 65, 66, 68, 70
Papists, 10, 35, 36, 68
Parable of the Wicked Mammon, The, 26
Parker, Matthew, 33, 34, 45, 47, 50, 63
Parker, Dr. T. H. L., 5, 71
Patrick, St., 66
Paul IV, pope, 41
Paul, St., 67
Peasants' Revolt, 29
Penry, John, 14
Persecution, religious, 30
Phocas, emperor, 17, 54
Pilgrim's Progress, 48
Platina's Lives of the Popes, 8
Practice of Prelates, The, 23, 26, 27, 31
Protestants, Protestantism, 12, 13, 21, 33, 44, 60, 64, 68, 69, 70
Puritan(s), 14, 26, 47, 48, 49

Reformation, the, 18, 21, 29, 48, 61, 64, 69, 71, 73
Reformers, Reformed Church, 9, 10, 11, 13, 14, 15, 16, 17, 18, 20, 23, 25, 27, 29, 51, 64, 69
  English, 24, 27, 30, 32, 44, 46, 52, 56, 64
  Magisterial, 11, 15, 16, 17, 18, 19, 20
  Radical, 15, 18, 19, 20
Renaissance, the, 69
Rerum Scoticarum Historia, 65
Revelation, Book of, 41, 42–3, 54, 74
Richard II, king, 25, 29
Richmond, duchess of, 34, 49
Rome, church of, 8, 10, 11, 12, 13, 17, 19, 34, 35, 36, 37, 39, 41, 43, 44, 47, 51, 52–3, 55, 57, 65, 66–7, 70

373

Royal supremacy, 37, 40

Saints' lives, 25, 39
Salesbury, William, 63-4
Sanctorum Angliae Catalogus, 39
Satan, 14, 40, 43, 54-5, 61
Saxons, 57, 63-4
Scriptures, 7, 8, 9, 10, 13, 16, 17, 18, 22, 23, 24, 26, 28, 30, 43, 49, 64, 70, 72
Scotland, 56, 63, 65
Severn, river, 22
Soames, Henry, 68
Spain, 14
Stillingfleet, Edward, 67
Switzerland, 11, 33
Sylvester I, pope, 41
    II, pope, 41

Theodore of Tarsus, 40
Thorpe, William, 30, 32, 44
Three Laws, The, 35
Tierney, M.A., 67
Tracts on the Origin . . . of the Ancient British Church, 68

Tudors, the, 40
Tudor England, 31, 44, 58, 59, 70
Tunstal, Cuthbert, 23
Tyndale, William, 22-32, 33, 42, 44, 51, 56

Ussher, James, 65-6, 67

Vergil, Polydore, 36-7, 38, 66, 69
Vitae Pontificum, 8, 41

Waldensians, 20, 56
Wales, Welsh, 30, 63-5
Wales, Marches of, 22
Wittenberg, 8, 22, 23
Word of God, 7, 9, 16, 24, 42
Worms, Diet of, 9
Wycliffe, John, 18, 20, 25, 29, 32, 44, 51, 54, 55, 56, 57-8, 61, 70
Wycliffites, 30

Zurich, 10
Zwingli, Huldreich, 10